Vegitalian

Italian Vegetarian Cooking

Floria Parmiani

Floria
PUBLICATIONS

ISBN 0-9653783-0-6

Library of Congress Catalog Card Number: 96-96908

Printed in the United States of America
First Edition

Book cover design by Al Fabrizio
Interior design by Al Fabrizio and Cheryl Fuller

Photography by Malcom Avery and Floria Parmiani

Front cover photograph: An *open market in Bologna (Emilia-Romagna).
In Italy, market places, shop windows and stalls are loaded with vegetables, flowers and fruits in a colorful confusion of nature gifts pouring out of a cornucopia. Everything is displayed in dramatic and artistic disorder. Spaghetti in sheaves are tied at the waist with white, red and green patriotic ribbons. *Fiaschi* of wine or olive oil are decorated with medals like war heroes. There are white cauliflowers from the north, green cauliflowers from Rome, and purple from Catania; short and green *zucchini* from everywhere or white and six-foot long *zucchini* from Naples; artichokes with thorns from the Riviera and without thorns from the south. There are pyramids of oranges, some sliced to show the bloody flesh preferred by Italians, and festoons of *caciocavalli* and *provoloni*; *mozzarelle* swimming in milk; pillars of *Parmigiano* cheese wheels painted funeral black; large jars of olives, mushrooms in oil, and pickled cucumbers.

Back cover photographs - (from left):

1. **Ponte della Pietra** (stone bridge) on the river Adige in Verona (Veneto). The bridge was built by the Romans during the second half of the 1st century B.C. Although it was destroyed during W.W.II, it has been rebuilt to its original design, using the antique stones, painstakingly retrieved along the river Adige.

2. **Piazza della Signoria, Florence** (Tuscany), and the football game, which is played the first Sunday in May and the 24th and 28th of June. The players are dressed in 16th century costumes. The Palazzo Vecchio (the old palace) stands majestic and severe in one of the most beautiful squares of Italy. It was built between the 13th and 14th centuries.

3. **Camogli** (Liguria). One of the "jewels" of the Italian Riviera.

To my daughter, Pucci,
with all my love and "mille grazie" for her faith in my work.

My Special Thanks

To my family, for teaching me the art and
appreciation of Italian cooking.

To Al Frabrizio, friend, mentor and collaborator
for helping me in the production and publication of this book.

To my friends, Wanda and Malcom Avery,
for sharing their photographs.

To my motivated and energetic students of Palo Alto, California,
for brainstorming the title of this book.

To Majorie Miller, Gail Fabrizio and Tara Milius,
for their editorial suggestions.

To my sister-in-law, Antonella Scardovi, for her famous recipes.

And to my many Italian friends, my sincere gratitude for their
invaluable teaching and for sharing their recipes.

ABOUT THE AUTHOR

Born and raised in Florence, Italy, Floria Parmiani is a writer, a painter, a sculptor and a teacher. She has authored two children's books, as well as numerous articles on Italian culture.

Her long time dream of publishing a book on Italian culture for travelers, is in process. This work grows out of a life-long understanding of her beloved Italy and a strong desire to share her knowledge with travelers everywhere. Floria Parmiani's plans include the publication of a collection of poems.

Other Books by Floria Parmiani
Classic Italian Tales/Novelline Italiane - a bilingual book for young children.
San Francisco in Colors - a historical coloring book.

TO ORDER THIS BOOK, OR OTHER BOOKS BY THE AUTHOR, CONTACT:

Floria Publications
773 Limerick Ct.
Sunnyvale, CA 94087-4743
Tel./Fax (408) 732-1588
e mail: floria@frabriziographics.com

Vegitalian

Italian Vegetarian Cooking

**Particular of "La Primavera"
(allegory of Spring), painted
by the Florentine Sandro
Botticelli in 1478. Uffizi
Gallery, Florence.**

Contents

Photographs:

Introduction

THE ITALIAN CUISINE

Italians know how to live well and one of the pleasures of life is eating well. Italians, like their art, are close to nature; and like nature, Italian food is vividly colored and fresh. The visual impact is as intense as the brilliant summer. Tomatoes, oranges, polished yellow, green and red peppers, green spinach, red radicchio, dark green lettuce, purple eggplants, black and green olives give each dish color and a simple, distinct taste.

Tasty food depends on the excellence of the ingredients that go into it. Italian food is harmonized with the fragrance of herbs and spices, the aromatic rosemary, sage, basil and thyme, fresh lemon juice, orange zest, and the spicy garlic, onions and leeks. Pure olive oil adds a wonderful flavor to dishes.

Good cooking begins in the market. Fruit and vegetables must be picked at the right time and they should not travel far. They must not be preserved by chemicals nor be refrigerated.

Red and white wines, produced in every Italian region, enrich each meal. Red wine must be served at room temperature, while white wine must be served chilled.

Food is good in Italy. It has character, and yet is seldom ambiguous or pretentious. The colors are gay: the yellow of the *risotto alla milanese*, or spaghetti with tomato sauce, the white of Tuscan beans, the gold of *fettuccine al doppio burro* are as pure as the colors of flags or children's crayons. Pizzas are painters' palettes ready to portray a summer sunset.

The recipes in this book reflect the Italian character: sparkling, colorful and artistic. Cook delicious dishes by using the best ingredients, as fresh as they can be found, and by following the easy directions for preparing each recipe.

VEGETARIAN ITALIAN STYLE

These recipes satisfy both the strict vegetarian who, like me, eat neither dairy products nor eggs, as well as those who include these products in their diet.

Good vegetarian food must appeal to both eye and taste. The recipes in this cookbook are of contrasting color and texture; they are special dishes in their unique simplicity and elegance. Menus are appropriate for everyday meals as well as for parties.

Each recipe requires 10 to 30 minutes for preparation unless slow cooking is specified. All the dishes share the same characteristics: They are tasty, nourishing and easy to prepare.

I have carefully selected and tested these recipes from Italian "trattorie,"* restaurants and friends. My family has cooked these dishes for many generations. The recipes in this book are the cooking from every Italian region.

* "Trattorie" are family-run, small restaurants. They usually serve the typical dishes of the region.

BACCHUS: *The Greek-Roman God of grape-growing and of wine. Painted by Caravaggio. Uffizi Gallery, Florence.*

Regional Cooking of Italy

Italy is distinguished by strong regional, historical and cultural differences. Its 20 regions (former independent states) are strongly individualistic. These regional divisions are especially manifested in food preparation. The most conspicuous differences are between the north and south. In the north, butter is the prevalent cooking fat; flat noodles (made with eggs,) are the pasta. In Tuscany and in the south, meals are cooked with olive oil. Tubular pasta, like macaroni and spaghetti, is used in the south; food in the southern regions is highly seasoned.

The true superiority of Italian food is in its vegetables and fruit. When asked the reason for the exquisite taste of these staples, Italians say it is because of the salt from sea mists, the different minerals of the land, the flowers, the climate, the soil and the absence of artificial fertilizers.

How about the distinct flavor of Italian food? It is in the art of cooking. Whatever Italians do is artistic: it is part of their heritage. Pasta, rice and vegetables are never overcooked. Italians cook their food "al dente" (slightly resistant to the teeth). They have introduced high quality herbs, spices and olive oil in the preparation of food, with true genius.

Rice is very important in the Italian cuisine. The Po River Valley in Lombardy, is the richest Italian agricultural region and the biggest rice producer in Europe. Rice grown in the northern region of Piedmont is superior to all other types grown in Italy.

Italy produces more than 40 varieties of pasta, usually made of very simple dough. The highest quality pasta is produced in the southern regions. This specialty derives from the purity of the mountain water.

There are several kinds of pastas:

Pasta for soup: Acini di pepe, anellini, conchigliette, semini di merlo, nocchette.

Pasta to be boiled: Spaghetti, fettuccine, lasagnette, ziti, capellini, fusilli, perciatelli, lingue di passero, mafaldine, fedelini.

Pasta for baking: lasagne, occhi di lupo, conchiglie, penne, farfalle, tortiglioni, grosso rigato, cappcllctti, ruote, spiedini, elbow macaroni.

Pasta to be stuffed: manicotti, cannelloni, ravioli, tortellini, agnolotti.

Polenta (cornmeal porridge) was a food of the first Romans. It was made from grain and served to nourish Roman soldiers. Boiled, it was eaten as porridge or hardened as a cake. Modern day polenta remains a national dish of Italy, especially in the north. It is still boiled, baked, fried and eaten warm or cold. Northern Italians are called "polentoni" for their extensive use of polenta in their cuisine. The finest polenta is grown in the Friuli-Venezia Giulia region. It is not the yellow polenta used in other northern regions, but a fine textured, white type, made from white corn.

Following is a list of some typical regional dishes presented in this book:

Piedmont: "Bagna cauda," rice with lemon, toast with hot melted cheese, garnished polenta.

Lombardy: Rice with saffron, braised peppers, poached egg soup, pears with Gorgonzola.

Northeast Regions: Braised rice and peas, radicchio (the king of lettuce, grown in Treviso), semolina dumplings with spinach, Macarpone cup.

Liguria: "Pesto," semolina dumplings.

Central Regions: Vegetable casserole, baked eggplant.

Tuscany: Beans and pasta, Florentine vegetable soup, white beans with tomatos, baked artichoke heart frittata.

Rome Regions: Noodles with butter and cheese, flakes of eggs and cheese, semolina cakes with butter and cheese, English soup.

Southern Regions: Tomato sauces, deep-fried Mozzarella sandwiches, marinated eggplants, cold eggplant, zabaglione.

Italy and Its Regions

Italy, including the islands of Sicily and Sardinia, is slightly larger than Arizona. The country is shaped like a boot. Italy's northwestern riviera, centered around Genoa, is washed by the Ligurian Sea while the country's western flank faces the Tyrrhenian Sea. From the heel to the toe, Italy has sandy and pebbly beaches on the Ionian Sea. The eastern shelf forms an unbroken sandy coastline along the Adriatic Sea.

The heel and some coastal areas are fairly low, but the country is generally mountainous. The Italian Alps and the Dolomiti mountains lie along the northern border, and the Appennini form a spine down the peninsula. Sicily and Sardinia are also rocky or mountainous.

Italy is divided into 20 regions, each having its unique history, culture and dialect, and each with a capital city. Regions are broken down into provinces, made up of many "comuni" (districts). Regions have a good measure of self-government under regional councils. The regions of Aosta, Trentino-Alto Adige, Sicily and Sardinia enjoy complete administrative autonomy. The capital of Italy is Rome.

The fertile Po river basin to the north holds some of Italy's richest farmland. Grapes have been harvested here from time immemorial and Italy produces about a quarter of the world's wines. Piedmont has the densest concentration of vineyards, especially in the provinces of Asti, Alessandria and Cuneo. The Tuscan Chianti and Sicilian Muscats and Marsala have a worldwide reputation.

Olive production is second only to that of Spain. About a third of the groves are in Apulia. The rice paddies of the well-watered plains of Piedmont and Lombardy, and those of Veneto and Emilia-Romagna, cover more than 100 square miles. The Mediterranean climate accounts for Italy being the second largest European producer of citrus fruits. The market is dominated by Sicily, which provides 90 percent of the lemons, 62 percent of the tangerines and 50 percent of the orange crop.

With the national diet based on pasta, it is hardly surprising that wheat is a basic crop. The hard grains used for pasta come in the greatest quantity from Sicily. The Parma area (Emilia-Romagna) is noted for its dairy products and food processing plants, with Parmigiano cheese having a worldwide reputation.

Italy

VALLEY OF AOSTA
• Aosta
Turin •
PEIDMONT

LOMBARDY
Milan •

ALTO ADIGE
Bolzano •
TRENTINO
Trento •
VENETO

FRIULI-VENETIA GIULIA
Trieste
Venice

EMILIA-ROMAGNA
Bologna •

Genoa
L I G U R I A

Florence •
TUSCANY

LIGURIAN SEA

THE MARCHE
Ancona •

A D R I A T I C   S E A

Perugia •
UMBRIA

LATIUM
★ ROME

L'Aquila •
ABRUZZI

MOLISE
Campobasso •

CAMPANIA

Naples •

Bari •
A P U L I A

BASILICATA
Potenza •

SARDINIA

TYRRHENIAN SEA

Cagliari

CALABRIA

Reggio Calabria

IONIAN SEA

Palermo •

MEDITERRANEAN SEA

SICILY

Wines of Italy

Italy produces hundreds of wines, from dry to sweet, and exports many of them to the United States. Because of the extraordinary range of wines, I have selected the best from vineyards of several Italian regions. You can enjoy many of these wines while visiting Italy.

Remember: Red wines must be served at room temperature, white wines are to be served chilled.

Asti Spumante: a sweet, sparkling wine from the town of Asti in Piedmont. This is not a classic Champagne-type wine. Note that "Champagne" is a French region.

Bardolino: from Lake Garda near Verona. A light red, dry wine with a spicy, bitter but pleasant flavor.

Barolo: from Piedmont. The finest Italian red wine. It is smooth, full-bodied and high in alcohol content. Buy this wine when it has aged more than three years; eight years is preferred.

Brolio: a fine wine from Tuscany. A red, rich and slightly flavored wine. It is the "Chianti classico" because it is produced in the "zona classica" of the Tuscan region.

Casteller: from Trentino-Alto Adige region. A white, light and dry wine with a fruity taste.

Cerasuolo del Piave: a strong rosé wine from Venice.

Chianti: associated with the classic Tuscan wine (Brolio). Even though it has a fruity fresh taste, this wine is not considered a Chianti classic.

Est! Est! Est!: (from Latin, It is! It is! It is!) This wine has its roots in Roman times. It is produced at Montefiascone, near Rome. A pleasant wine, it can be slightly tart or semisweet.

Frascati: from Rome. A very unpredictable wine, sometimes dry, sometimes semisweet. When it is good, it has a straw color and a mellow, refreshing taste.

Freisa: from Piedmont. A red wine with a touch of sharpness, but not tart taste. It has a refreshing fruity flavor.

Grignolino: from Piedmont. Its pleasant and nutty flavor makes it one of the most delicate Italian red wines.

Mamertino: a Sicilian sweet wine which was praised by Julius Caesar and the poet Martial.

Marsala: from the city in Sicily. There are two types of Marsala, sweet and dry. It has a moscato taste. The sweet Marsala is served with dessert; the dry type is used for cooking.

Merlot: from Trentino-Alto Adige region. This red wine is warm and slightly piquant.

Nebbiolo: from Piedmont. Lighter than Barolo, it is full-bodied with an aroma of violets.

Orvieto: from Umbria. A pleasant, white and fruity wine. It can be either dry or semisweet. It is usually served with desserts.

Ravello Rosato: from Salerno near Naples. A delicate sweet rosé. Its fruity flavor makes a refreshing companion to desserts.

Soave: from the region near Verona. It is the finest Italian white wine. Mild and delicate, it has a distinctive bouquet you will never forget.

Valpolicella: from Verona. A dark red, mellow wine with enough body to be served with the most formal meals.

Verdicchio dei Castelli di Jesi: from the Marche. A white, dry wine with a slightly bitter taste. It is considered a superior table wine.

Vermouth: from Piedmont, it is the great aperitivo of Italy. This wine, which is made of blended wines, spirits, herbs and bitters, may be served either chilled or at room temperature.

Vino Santo Toscano: from Florence. A simple wine pressed by every farmer, who jealously guards his wine-producing efforts.

Cheeses of Italy

Italians eat very little meat and display little interest in fresh milk. Much of the milk goes into cheese which is the pride of Italy. Practically every region produces a distinct cheese and a great deal of attention is devoted to the art of cheese making.

There are hundreds of cheese varieties with a national and international reputation for excellence. Like wines, cheeses enhance the quality of Italian meals. Cheese appears in every Italian menu: in soups, salads, pasta and vegetables, as well as a companion of fruits and wines.

When cooking with cheese, buy Italian imported products. Domestic cheeses lack distinct taste, texture and flavor. Below is a list of the finest cheeses produced in Italy; many of them are available in the United States.

TABLE CHEESES

Asiago: from the province of Vicenza (Veneto). A sharp, hard and granular cheese, made from two cow milkings. One milking is skimmed, the other is partly skimmed.

Bel Paese: from Lombardy. A soft, smooth yellow cheese; it is deliciously flavored.

Fontina: a product of the Valle d'Aosta. This fine cheese is semisoft, delicate and sweet.

Gorgonzola: originally from a town in the Alpine area near Milan. Now it is produced in the Po river flatlands. Ranked among the finest veined cheeses, it is sharp and lightly spiced.

Mascarpone: from the region of Lombardy. A fresh creamy cheese eaten for dessert, sometimes with powdered chocolate, sometimes with Maraschino and sugar.

Pecorino: from the towns of Accumoli and Vallecupola in the province of Rieti (near Rome). Pecorino is a very old cheese, produced since early Roman times. It is firm and sharp and can be grated as well as eaten as a table cheese. Pecorino is from whole sheep's milk.

Provolone: from Naples. A variety of Cacciocavallo. For two or three months, this product is creamy and delicate; thereafter, sharp and spicy.

Ricotta: from the province of Rome. A very old cheese dating from the Roman time. This moist, fresh, unsalted cheese is used in sandwitches, salads and blintzes. Mixed with Marsala wine, it is a deliciously flavored dessert.

Robiole: from the towns of Roccaverano and Marazzano in Piedmont. This cheese is spicy and creamy.

Taleggio: originally produced in Bergamo (Lombardy), is from dry, salted curds with an aromatic flavor.

Toma Veja: from Gressoney Valley in Piedmont. A heavy cheese with a reddish crust, derived from fermentation.

COOKING CHEESES

Mozzarella: from Naples. Made from buffalo or cow milk, this cheese has a mellow, slightly sour flavor. It is used on pizza and mixed with ricotta, in lasagne. It can be eaten by itself at the end of a meal.

Prescinseua: from Genoa. A sour cheese from milk curds; it is used in vegetable dishes.

Provatura: from the province of Rome. A cheese which melts easily in the oven. "Crostini alla provatura" are slices of bread topped with Provatura which, when placed in the oven, envelops the bread.

GRATING CHEESES

Casu Marzu: from the area of Gallura in Sardinia. It is a delicious grana-type cheese Sardinians eat with their pasta.

Parmigiano Reggiano: produced in small towns of northern Italy. This cheese is considered the world's true seasoning cheese. Made only from April to November under carefully controlled conditions, this product is salty and sharp. It should be grated just before serving. Freshly cut and moist, it can be used as a table cheese.

Pecorino Romano: assertive taste, made of fresh sheep's milk. It is used on pasta or as a table cheese.

Fine Herbs and Spices

No Italian kitchen is without fresh or dried herbs and spices. They enrich and diversify the flavor of many dishes. When you go shopping, look for Italian herbs, spices and olive oil. Buy all you need to cook "Vegitalian!"

Here is a list of fine herbs and their use. A note of caution: Dry mint, parsley, basil and sage have a bitter taste. Use them infrequently.

Basil: An annual plant cultivated in Western Europe. Best when used fresh. Leaves may be dried, ground and powdered. Use in soups, sauces; with cucumbers, peas, potatoes, salad greens, squash and in combination with tomatoes.

Bay Leaf: The aromatic leaf of the sweet-bay or laurel tree. Use dry or whole in soups, potatoes, beets, carrots and tomatoes.

Caraway: A biennial herb with an aromatic fruit known as caraway seeds. It is sold whole or ground. Use in breads, cookies, cakes, candies, salads, cheese, beets, broccoli, Brussel sprouts, cabbage, carrots, cauliflower, onions and potatoes.

Cayenne Pepper: Sometimes called red pepper. Powdered pod and seeds of various capsicums yielding a hot, savory flavor. Grown mainly in Africa. Use in gravies.

Celery Seeds: Seed of a small plant similar in appearance and taste to celery. Southern France, India and the United States are producers. Use whole or ground in soups, cheese, pickles, some salads, cabbage, potatoes.

Cervil: A celery like plant with aromatic leaves. Use in soups and salads.

Chives: Similar to green onions, but smaller and milder. Use in cottage and cream cheeses, scrambled eggs and cream soups.

Cinnamon: The original cinnamon is from the inner bark of Cinnamon zeylancium which grows only in Ceylon. It has a very mild flavor. Cassia cinnamon, grown also in the Far East, is commonly marketed in the United States. This type has a more full-bodied flavor. It is sold in sticks or ground. Use in cakes, grapefruit and melon.

Cloves: The flower buds of a tree which is grown in India, Zanzibar and Madagascar. Sold whole or ground.

Coriander: An herb with aromatic seeds. Use in cookies, pickles potatoes, breads and salad.

Curry: A yellow condiment from India containing various spices. Use in egg dishes.

Dill: An annual herb grown for its aromatic seed. It is cultivated mostly in India. Use in pickles, sauces, creamed potatoes, coleslaw, sour cream sauces, potatoes, beets, broccoli, Brussel sprouts, cabbage, carrots, cauliflower, cucumbers, peas and salad greens.

Fennel: The seeds of this herb are ground. Fennel resembles celery in appearance and has a fragrance and taste suggestive of anise. Use it ground in sauces and apple pie; use the young stalks in salads. In Italy it is served like celery.

Garlic: A strong flavored plant of the lily family. Cloves are used to flavor all types of vegetable foods.

Ginger: The root of an herbaceous grown in semi-tropical countries. Black ginger is from an unscraped root stock. It is a must in many desserts and sour cream.

Leeks: Strong flavored plant similar to onion. Use in vegetable soups and salads.

Marjoram: A fragrant annual of the mint family. Leaves are dried and sold whole or powdered. Use in soups, salads, mushrooms, scrambled eggs, omelets, rice, beans, carrots and peas.

Mint: A fragrant plant; its leaves are sold whole or powdered. Use fresh in soups, beans, cabbage, carrots, cucumbers, peas, fruits and beverages.

Mustard: The seeds of this plant are sold whole or ground. Use in pickles, salads, scrambled eggs, cheese sauce, asparagus, beans, broccoli, cabbage, onions, potatoes and squash.

Nutmeg: The kernel of the fruit of the Myristica tree grown in India. The fruit resembles an apricot in shape and size. It has four parts: the outer husk, the mace, the inner shell and the seed or nutmeg. It is sold whole or ground. Use in creamed onions, carrots, cabbage, spinach, sweet potatoes and canned peaches.

Olive Oil: Made from the flesh of ripe olives. Extra virgin olive oil is that which is first extracted. It is superior in flavor and appearance than the oil produced by the second (virgin olive oil) or third (pure olive oil) pressing. The best olive oil in the world comes from Italy. The finest comes from Lucca, in Tuscany, and from Sassari, in Sardinia.

Onion: A strong flavored plant of the lily family. Use in most vegetable dishes.

Oregano: It is a favorite of Italian cooks. It gives character to potatoes, tomatoes, baked beans, eggplant, onions, peas and spinach.

Paprika: A sweet red pepper which is dried and ground after seeds and stems are removed. It has a mild flavor. Use in salad dressings, salads and vegetables.

Parsley: A biennial herb. Use in vegetable dishes and salad; also as a garnish.

Pepper: Made from peppercorns which are the dried berries of a vine. White pepper is made from what is left of the fully ripened berry after the outer coat has been removed.

Rosemary: An evergreen plant. Its leaves and flowers are used in sauces, dumplings, biscuits, cauliflower and corn.

Saffron: A flower similar to a crocus. It has a rich orange-yellow color. Use in rice and breads.

Sage: A perennial mint. Leaves are best when used fresh in soups, sauces, Brussel sprouts, peas, onions and tomatoes.

Scallions: Small onions.

Tabasco Sauce: A highly seasoned sauce made with cayenne peppers and other ingredients.

Tarragon: A perennial herb. Use leaves in asparagus, beans, broccoli, cabbage, cauliflower, cucumbers, salad greens, pickles and vinegar.

Thyme: An herb. Its powdered leaves are used in tomatoes, potatoes, onions, carrots, Brussel sprout, beets and beans.

Truffles: Italians call the truffle "the diamond of the table." Having no chlorophyll, this unusual fungus must grow with some other vegetation. Truffles grow underground in the root systems of certain kinds of trees. In Piedmont, they grow under hazels, oaks, poplars, chestnuts and willows at an altitude of 1,400-1,980 feet. Truffles do not grow above the ground; to find them dogs are trained to sniff them out. The Piedmont truffle, from the Langhe Valley, is of a rare whiteness and most prized for its strong flavor. Black truffles are less valued.

Helpful Hints

1. **Diversify Your Diet.** Prepare different dishes every day; let two or three weeks elapse before you use the same dish. Even the best food is spoiled by boredom.

2. If you are a strict vegetarian, substitute **Extra Virgin Olive Oil** for butter in the same proportion whenever possible. Also, use **Vegetable Bouillon** instead of milk and **Yogurt** instead of cream.

3. To cut down on cholesterol, use **Eggs Substitute** products. Use the recommended 1/4 cup = 1 egg.

4. Use **Sea Salt** instead of regular salt. It is healthier and it gives a better taste to your food. But use it sparingly.

5. **Garlic.** It is less acrid and more digestible when you crush the clove and remove it before serving.

6. **Dry Herbs and Spices.** They are very useful to enrich food. Dry herbs, aromatic seeds and spices used in this book are: pepper (white and black), nutmeg, cinnamon, oregano, thyme, cayenne pepper, dragoncello, curry, cloves, saffron, marjoram, mustard, cumin seeds, fennel seeds and laurel. However, I rarely use dry parsley, mint, basil or sage, preferring them fresh.

7. **How to Peel Tomatoes.** Bring to boil a full pot of water. Remove from the stove. Place tomatoes in water for 30 seconds continually turning them. Place them in cold water; peel.

8. **Do Not Store Warm Food In The Refrigerator.** Vapors cause the spreading of odors to other foods.

9. **Do not store potatos, onions or bananas** in the refrigerator.

10. To retain their freshness, **keep vegetables refrigerated no longer than two days.**

11. **High heat cooking** is the enemy of successful cuisine.

12. **When adding liquid** to recipes, always use small, warm quantities.

13. A pan should be large enough to hold its contents comfortably. Heavy pans heat slowly and cook food at a constant rate. Enamelware is a poor conductor of heat. Aluminum and cast iron conduct heat well but may discolor foods containing egg yolks, wine, vinegar or lemon. **The best pans are stainless steel or enameled cast iron.**

The Secret of Your Success in Cooking

Cooking is not an exact science. The amount required for any recipe is never precise; my suggestion is to taste and adjust the recipe to your preference. Tasting for seasoning is the secret of your success in cooking.

UNLESS OTHERWISE SPECIFIED, RECIPES IN THIS BOOK SERVE FOUR PEOPLE.

SOGLIO (Piedmont). *This picturesque village, near the western Alps, is in the province of Asti. This area is well-known for its wines: the sparkling Asti Spumante; the ruby-red strong Barbera and the clear garnet red Grignolino.*

Sauces

If you like to eat well, add sauces to your recipes.
They will transform a simple dish into a delicious meal.

Unless otherwise specified,
recipes in this book serve four people.

BESCIAMELLA

1 teaspoon butter, or 1 teaspoon pure olive oil 1 tablespoon flour milk, as needed	Dash sea salt Dash nutmeg Few grains pepper

1. Melt butter in a small pan; do not brown. Add flour and blend well.

2. Over medium-high heat, cook for 3-5 minutes stirring briskly.

3. Add milk, slowly, stirring briskly; add salt, nutmeg and pepper as desired. Add more milk only when previous liquid is completely absorbed.

4. Lower heat and cook for 7-10 minutes, stirring occasionally, as needed.

Taste for seasoning. Sauces requiring Besciamella (see following recipes), are served warm.

SALSA MAITRE-D'HOTEL
Chef Sauce

Blend 1 cup Besciamella (see page 1) with:

1 teaspoon butter,
    or 2 teaspoons pure olive oil
1 tablespoon fresh parsley, minced

1 (medium) lemon juice
    (optional)

Taste for seasoning; serve warm with vegetables.

SALSA MORNEY
Besciamella and Cheese Sauce

Prepare a double recipe of Besciamella (see page 1) but substitute milk with 1/4 cup cream. Then blend 16 oz. Besciamella with:

2 oz. butter, or 3 tablespoons pure olive oil
2 oz. freshly grated Parmigiano or Gruviera
    (or a mix of two cheeses)

Taste for seasoning, and serve warm with vegetables. Also serve with soft boiled eggs (see page 61).

SALSA ALLA PANNA
Cream Sauce

To 1 cup Besciamella (see page 1) add and blend:

1/3 cup hot cream
Few drops lemon juice (optional)

Taste for seasoning; serve warm with vegetables. Without lemon juice, serve warm with hot hard boiled eggs.

SALSA AURORA

Besciamella and Tomato Sauce

To 1 cup warm Besciamella (see page 1), add and blend:

1 tablespoon tomato sauce
1 teaspoon butter, or 2 teaspoons pure olive oil
1 tablespoon freshly grated Parmigiano cheese

Taste for seasoning; serve warm with boiled artichokes, hot hard boiled eggs or soft boiled eggs (see page 61).

SALSA ANDALUSA

Besciamella and Herbs Sauce

To 1 cup Besciamella (see page 1) or White Sauce (see page 5), add and blend:

1 tablespoon tomato sauce
1 tablespoon minced fresh parsley
2 tablespoons sweet pepper, coarsely chopped and
     cooked slowly in a little butter
1 clove garlic (optional), well crushed (remove before serving).

Taste for seasoning; serve warm with hard boiled eggs or soft boiled eggs (see page 61).

SALSA ALLE UOVA

Egg Sauce

To 1 cup warm Besciamella (see page 1), carefully add and blend:

2 hard boiled eggs, finely chopped
1 tablespoon fresh parsley, minced

Taste for seasoning; serve warm as a side dish.

SALSA SOUBISE (1)

Besciamella and Wine Sauce (1)

1 cup Besciamella   **8 oz. dry white wine**
1 large onion, sliced or minced   **3-4 tablespoons cream**

1. Cook onion in wine for 30 minutes. Crush onion in a dish with fork, or use blender.

2. Prepare a thick Besciamella sauce (see page 1). Then, over low heat, add onion mixture and cream. Add salt to taste.

Taste for seasoning; serve with steamed vegetables or soft boiled eggs. (see page 61).

SALSA RAVIGOTTA

Flavored Besciamella Sauce

1 cup Besciamella
1 teaspoon butter,
   or 2 teaspoons pure olive oil
2 tablespoons cream
1/3 cup vinegar
1/3 cup dry white wine

1/2 small onion, sliced
1 sprig rosemary (or a pinch
   of dry, powdered thyme)
1 bay leaf
Few grains fresh black pepper

1. In a small saucepan, combine all ingredients except Besciamella, butter and cream. Bring to a boil and simmer until liquid is reduced to half the amount. Strain.

2. Prepare Besciamella sauce (see page 1) . Then, combine with aromatic liquid previously prepared. Cook over very low heat 5 minutes, stirring as needed.

3. Remove from heat; add butter and cream; salt to taste.

Taste for seasoning; serve with soft boiled eggs (see page 61).

SALSA BIANCA O VELLUTATA

White Sauce

Prepare a Besciamella sauce (see page 1), but substitute vegetable bouillon for milk. Use this sauce to enhance other sauces (see below).

SALSA ALLA PAPRIKA
Paprika Sauce

2 oz. butter, or
   3 tablespoons pure olive oil
1 tablespoon flour
1 small onion, minced

2 cups (or more)
   vegetable bouillon
Pinch paprika

1. With 1 oz. butter, cook onion over very low heat; cover. When onion is transparent, but not brown, add flour, stir constantly for 2-5 minutes.

2. Slowly, add bouillon until sauce begins to thicken.

3. Cook over very low heat for 10 more minutes, stirring occasionally.

4. Remove from heat, add remaining butter and paprika. Salt, if necessary.

Taste for seasoning; serve with hot soft boiled eggs (see page 61).

SALSA AL FORMAGGIO
Cheese Sauce

3 tablespoons butter,
   or 4 tablespoons pure olive oil
3 tablespoons flour
1 1/4 cup vegetable bouillon
1 cup cream

4 tablespoons Parmigiano
   or Gruviera cheese, grated
Sea salt to taste
Nutmeg (pinch)
Pepper (optional)

1. With butter, flour and bouillon, prepare a White Sauce (see page 5).

2. Over very low heat, add cream, stirring briskly; cook 5-7 minutes longer.

3. Keep heat on low, add cheese, salt, pepper, nutmeg. Remove from heat when cheese is melted.

Taste for seasoning; serve with steamed vegetables or soft boiled eggs (see page 61).

MAYONNAISE SAUCE

Use a good commercial Mayonnaise.

SALSA MOUSSELINE
Mayonnaise and Cream Sauce (1)

Combine Mayonnaise with whipped cream (unsweetened). The proportions vary depending on your taste; however, the whipped cream and Mayonnaise should be mixed in equal amounts. Combine just before serving.

Taste for seasoning; serve with asparagus, cold vegetables, and cold hard boiled eggs.

SALSA CHANTILLY
Mayonnaise and Cream Sauce (2)

Just before serving, combine Mayonnaise with whipped cream (unsweetened) and some egg whites, beaten stiff.

Taste for seasoning; serve with asparagus, cold vegetables, or cold hard boiled eggs.

SALSA MALTESE

Mayonnaise and Orange Juice Sauce

Combine 1 cup Mayonnaise with:

Juice of 1/2 orange
Pinch of saffron

OR

Combine 1 cup Mayonnaise with:

Juice of 1/2 orange
1 teaspoon thinly sliced orange zest

Before blending with Mayonnaise, cook orange zest 2 minutes in boiling water; dry well.

Taste for seasoning; serve with cold asparagus.

ROUILLE

Mayonnaise and Lemon

1 cup Mayonnaise with
   1 tablespoon lemon juice
1 slice Italian or French bread

1/2 teaspoon paprika
1 tablespoon pure olive oil
Pinch of garlic, minced

Remove bread crust; place slice of bread in cold water; squeeze water out. Mix with the other ingredients, except oil. Then add oil and blend carefully.

Taste for seasoning; serve with steamed vegetables, boiled potatoes, or hard boiled eggs.

SALSA ALLA MOSTARDA

Cream and Mustard Sauce

1 teaspoon mustard   **Sea salt to taste**
1 teaspoon lemon juice **Pepper**
8 oz. cream

Blend mustard with lemon juice, add cream, slowly. Add salt and pepper.

Taste for seasoning; serve with cold asparagus, or cold boiled artichokes.

SALSA GOLF

Golf Sauce

Combine:

6 tablespoons Mayonnaise   **Few drops of tobasco (optional)**
2 tablespoons heavy cream sauce   **Few drops of Worcestershire**
1 teaspoon ketchup   **Sea salt (if needed)**
1 teaspoon lemon juice   **Pepper (optional)**

Taste for seasoning; serve with cold hard boiled eggs; or fill halved avocados.

SALSA SOUBISE (2)

Tomato and Vinegar Sauce (2)

2 1/4 cups onions, sliced
2 oz. butter, or
   3 tablespoons pure olive oil
1 tablespoon vinegar
1 tablespoon Italian
   tomato paste (Pomi brand)

Sea salt to taste
Pinch of sugar
Dry, white wine

1. Place onions in small saucepan with butter. Add equal parts of water and wine, enough to barely cover onions. Bring to a boil, lower heat, simmer over very low heat for 1/2 hour. If necessary, cook over high heat until liquid is absorbed.

2. Put this mixture in blender; add tomato paste, salt, vinegar and sugar. Blend all ingredients. Taste for seasoning; flavor must be well balanced.

3. Refrigerate, covered, until ready to serve. Serve with steamed vegetables, hard boiled eggs, or soft boiled eggs (see page 61).

SKORDALIA

Almond Sauce

Combine:

1 cup pure olive oil
1-2 garlic cloves, minced
2 oz. almonds,
   peeled and minced
2 tablespoons fresh
   Italian parsley, chopped
1 large boiled potato, cut up

1 thick slice Italian or
   French bread, soaked in
   cold water, well squeezed
3 tablespoons vinegar
Sea salt
Black pepper

Process all ingredients in blender until smooth. Taste for seasoning; serve with raw tomatoes.

TOMATO SAUCES

See Pasta chapter pages 71, 72.

VINAIGRETTE SAUCE

Use this sauce with salads and steamed vegetables. It is prepared with pure olive oil and vinegar. For 4 people, the normal amount is 6 tablespoons of oil and 2 tablespoons of vinegar.

When you prepare it, remember to add sea salt before the oil because salt does not dissolve in cold oil. Mix the ingredients well (salt, pepper and vinegar) before pouring over salad; then add and toss with olive oil.

VINAIGRETTE CURRY

Mix Vinaigrette sauce with:

1 teaspoon powdered curry
1 small leek, minced

CREAM VINAIGRETTE

Substitute cream for pure olive oil. Taste for seasoning; serve with salad or cold cooked vegetables.

CITRONNETTE

Mix well:

3 parts pure olive oil
1 part lemon juice
Sea salt

Pepper
Fresh parsley, minced

Taste for seasoning; serve with salad, or vegetables, cold or warm.

CITRONNETTE AND HARD BOILED EGG

Mix:

6 tablespoons pure olive oil
1-2 tablespoons lemon juice

Sea salt
Pepper

Blend in 1 hard boiled egg yolk, crushed with a fork. Taste for seasoning; serve with salad.

CREAMY CITRONNETTE

Substitute cream for olive oil. Taste for seasoning; serve with salad.

CAMOGLI (Liguria): One of the treasures of the Eastern Italian Riviera in the Gulf of Genoa. The little port of this charming village is surrounded by six-storied apartment houses faced with colored plaster. These buildings look like they have been dabbed by a 19th century impressionist painter. Camogli is a harmonious mix of fishing nets, sails, boat hulls and flowered balconies.

PORTOFINO (Liguria). *Toward the East of the Genoa coast, the Riviera del Levante reveals the spell of its enchantment: the mountain of Portofino. Called "pearl of the world" because of its natural beauty, this village is situated in the Southern extremity of the Tigullio Gulf. Built around a natural harbor and reaching well into the "piazzetta," or little square, this village is one of the most cherished meeting places of cosmopolitan tourism, one of the most famous resorts of the world, a meeting place for yachts from all over the world.*

Antipastos

Antipastos may also be served as companions to main dishes.

Always taste recipes for seasoning or flavor.

Unless otherwise specified,
recipes in this book serve four people.

AVOCADO

Like the melon, avocado is an easy dish to prepare. It is also inexpensive. Buy a soft but firm fruit. To ripen fruit, store at room temperature until soft. To speed ripening, put avocados in a paper bag with an apple or banana until soft. Prepare the avocado just before serving.

Below are the simplest recipes:

1. Cut the fruit in half, remove the stone; fill the cavities with pure olive oil, salt and black pepper.

2. Prepare as above, but fill the cavities with a Vinaigrette sauce (olive oil, vinegar, salt, black pepper) or Citronnette sauce (olive oil, juice of 1 lemon, salt, black pepper). To the Vinaigrette or Citronnette sauces you may add a few drops of tobasco.

3. Peel the avocado, cut in half, remove the stone. Cut fruit in small regular pieces. Dress with pure olive oil, salt, black pepper, vinegar or lemon juice and a few drops of tobasco.

AVOCADO, TOMATOES AND LEMON

Serves 6

1. Peel, cut in half, then make horizontal slices of 2 avocados.

2. Cut 3 tomatoes in eight vertical segments.

3. Peel and slice 1 lemon. (Remove the white inner layer.)

4. Place all ingredients in a large dish and dress with the juice and grated zest of the lemon (do not grate the white inner layer of lemon). Beat 4 tablespoons pure olive oil, Sea salt and black pepper. Pour over avocado and tomato mixture.

5. Refrigerate 30 minutes before serving. Accompany dish with black bread.

BREAD AND CHEESE

With a fork, mix 3 parts of Mascarpone, 1 tablespoon butter and 2 tablespoons sharp Gorgonzola.

Spread over slices of brown bread; top with walnut quarters.

BROAD BEANS AND CHEESE

Beans must be very young and very fresh. Serve with fresh Pecorino (from Sardinia or Rome).

MELON

Melons are very pleasant antipastos, especially in summer. They are also easy to prepare. They are served cold, but must not be refrigerated too long.

Slice and sprinkle with fresh mint, or powdered ginger.

MELON AND PORTO, MARSALA, OR SHERRY

For antipasto, as well as dessert, serve small melons cut in half. Discard seeds and filaments. Remove pulp in small balls or squares; soak with sugar (scant) and Porto, dry Marsala, or Sherry. Taste for flavoring.

Refrigerate. Fill melon rinds and serve with dessert spoons.

MELON AND GRUVIERA

1. Cut approximately 1 1/2 inch from the stem side of a large melon, or cut small melons in half. Discard seeds and filaments; remove pulp and make small balls or squares.

2. Mix an equal quantity of Gruviera and melon; add Kirsch or Rum and a few grains of pepper. Taste for flavoring.

3. Fill empty rinds with melon balls, cover the top. Refrigerate. Before serving, add a few grains of Sea salt.

STUFFED TOMATOES

1. Wash and dry tomatoes; cut in half horizontally; squeeze slightly to eliminate seeds and water. Sprinkle the inside of tomatoes with Sea salt and place face down for 1 hour.

2. Stuff tomatoes with Mayonnaise blended with thin slices of celery, finely chopped hard boiled eggs, a few drops of Worcestershire sauce, thick cream and lemon if desired. Taste for seasoning.

SALTED CANAPES

You can buy excellent cocktail canapes and stuff them with:

a. A blend of 2 parts Mascarpone, 1 part butter, 1 part sharp Gorgonzola and a few drops of dry Marsala.

b. Mix equal parts of Mascarpone, salted, roasted almonds (finely chopped), chopped pickled gherkins. Top with a slice of gherkins.

Instead of canapes, you may use whole wheat crackers.

COLD VEGETABLES

Cold vegetables are excellent antipastos. Some examples are: carrots with olive oil and lemon; asparagus and raw artichokes in Citronnette Sauce; boiled cold artichokes in Cream and Mustard Sauce; radish; Mushroom Salad; Mushrooms with Cognac.

For these recipes, see individual listing.
— Citronette Sauce, page 12.
— Cream and Mustard Sauce, page 9.
— Raw Mushroom Salad, page 125.
— Cold Mushroom with Cognac, page 101.

MARINATED MUSHROOMS

Makes 2 cups

2/3 cup pure olive oil
1/2 cup water
Juice of 2 lemons
1 bay leaf
2 garlic cloves, crushed

6 whole peppercorns
Sea salt
1 pound small whole
    fresh mushrooms

1. Combine olive oil, water, lemon juice, bay leaf, garlic, peppercorns and salt in a 10 or 12-inch skillet, and bring to a boil over moderate heat.

2. Reduce heat, cover and simmer 15 minutes. Strain through sieve and return liquid to skillet; bring to a simmer over low heat.

3. Drop mushrooms into marinade and simmer for 5 minutes, stirring them occasionally.

4. Cool marinated mushrooms. Serve at room temperature or, after they have cooled, refrigerate and serve cold. (Mushrooms will keep in refrigerator at least 2 days).

5. If served cold, lift mushrooms out of marinade with a slotted spoon; drain carefully; arrange them on a platter or in a serving bowl.

MARINATED EGGPLANT

Makes 4 cups

3 quarts water
1 to 1 1/2 pounds eggplant,
   unpeeled, cut into
   1-inch cubes (about 6 cups)
1/4 cup wine vinegar
1/2 teaspoon finely
   chopped garlic
1/2 teaspoon dry basil,
   crumbled

1/2 teaspoon dry oregano,
   crumbled
Sea salt
1/8 teaspoon coarsely
   ground black pepper
1/4 cup pure olive oil

1. Bring water to a boil over high heat in a large saucepan. Drop in eggplant, reduce heat and simmer uncovered 10 minutes, or until eggplant can be easily pierced with tip of a sharp knife.

2. Drain in large sieve, pat dry with paper towel.

3. Mix vinegar, garlic, basil, oregano, salt and pepper in large bowl. Add eggplant and toss ingredients gently until coated with vinegar and herbs.

4. Marinate in refrigerator for 1 hour. Before serving, toss eggplant with olive oil.

CAPONATA
Cold Eggplant

2 pounds eggplant,
   peeled and cut into
   1/2-inch cubes (8 cups)
1/2 cup pure olive oil
2 cups finely chopped celery
3/4 cup finely chopped onion
1/3 cup wine vinegar mixed
   with 4 teaspoons sugar

3 cups drained
   canned Italian tomatoes
2 tablespoons Italian
   tomato paste (Pomi brand)
6 large green olives, well
   rinsed, pitted, and slivered
Sea salt
Freshly grounded black pepper
2 tablespoons pine nuts

1. Sprinkle cubes of eggplant generously with salt and set them in a colander or large sieve over paper towel to drain. After 30 minutes, pat cubes dry with fresh paper towels and set them aside.

2. In a heavy 14-inch skillet, heat 1/4 cup pure olive oil. Add celery and cook over moderate heat, stirring frequently for 10 minutes.

3. Add onions and cook 8 to 10 minutes, or until celery and onions are soft and slightly colored. With slotted spoon, transfer them to a bowl.

4. Pour remaining 1/4 cup olive oil into skillet, add eggplant and sauté over high heat, stirring and turning them constantly for 8 minutes, or until lightly brown.

5. Return celery and onions to skillet and stir in vinegar and sugar, drained tomatoes, tomato paste, green olives, 1/2 teaspoon of salt and a few grindings of pepper.

6. Bring to a boil, reduce heat, simmer uncovered, stirring frequently for 15 minutes. Stir in pine nuts.

7. Taste for seasoning. Transfer Caponata to a serving bowl and refrigerate until ready to serve.

GARNISHED POLENTA

For preparation of Polenta, page 56.

4 slices polenta
4 slices Fontina cheese
1 can white truffles (see page xxi)
Pure olive oil as needed

1. Fry polenta slices in pure olive oil. Cool. Place a slice of Fontina over each slice of polenta.

2. Bake in moderate oven until cheese is soft. Garnish each slice with truffles.

CHEESE BALLS

4 1/2 oz. Gruviera or
    Parmigiano cheese,
    freshly grated
2 egg whites

Tomato sauce
    (see pages 71, 72)
Pure olive oil

1. Beat egg whites until stiff. Carefully fold in cheese.

2. Form small balls the size of a walnut; fry in oil (the balls will rise to the size of tangerines.)

3. Pour tomato sauce over fried cheese balls. Serve hot.

BAGNA CAUDA

Garlic Dip   *Serves 6*

THE VEGETABLES:
1 green pepper, cleaned and seeded, cut into 1/2 inch strips,
   2 inches long
1 red pepper, cleaned and seeded, cut into 1/2 inch strips,
   2 inches long
4 celery stalks, cut into 1/2 inch strips, 2 inches long
1 cucumber, peeled and seeded, cut into 1/2 inch strips,
   2 inches long
2 carrots, peeled and cut into 1/2 inch strips, 2 inches long
1 bunch scallions, trimmed and cut into 2-inch lengths
1/2 pound fresh small mushrooms, whole
1 small head of romaine lettuce, broken into separate leaves
10 cherry tomatoes
Italian bread sticks

FOR THE DIP:
1 teaspoon finely chopped garlic   1 can white truffles,
4 tablespoons butter   finely chopped
2 cups heavy cream

1. Soak vegetables strips in a bowl of ice cubes and water for 1 hour.

2. Pat vegetables dry with towel and arrange on a serving dish with lettuce leaves, mushrooms and tomatoes. Cover with plastic wrap and refrigerate.

3. In a heavy enameled saucepan, bring the cream to a boil and cook for 15-20 minutes, stirring frequently, until it has thickened.

4. Use a 4-cup flameproof earthenware casserole to fit over a candle warmer or electric hot tray. On the stove, melt butter in the casserole over low heat (do not brown!) Add garlic, the thickened cream and truffles. Bring the sauce to a simmer, stirring constantly. (Do not boil!) Serve at once.

5. To serve, keep Bagna Cauda warm over a candle warmer or electric hot tray. Accompany sauce with cold vegetables and bread sticks.

6. To eat, dip vegetable or bread stick into hot sauce. If butter and cream separate, beat with a whisk.

Variations for raw vegetables: cauliflower, broccoli, fennels, white turnip, radishes (red or white).

VERNAZZA (Liguria): One of the villages along the unusual zone known as the "Cinque Terre" (Five Lands) in the Gulf of La Spezia (the "Gulf of the Poets"). Vernazza is built in a little cove which once was an anchorage for Roman cargo vessels. It has narrow streets and old houses huddling together on a rocky promontory. The "Cinque Terre" are: Monterosso, Vernazza, Corniglia, Manarola and Riomaggiore. This is the Italian Riviera that fascinated Italian, English, German and French Romantics. It is one of the most untouched and gentle coasts of the Mediterranean.

Vegetable Creams

In summer, vegetable creams can be served cold, using yogurt instead of cream. If you prefer, you may eliminate the croutons, but keep the cream thick. I do not use eggs in the preparation; instead, I double the quantity of cream.

Unless otherwise specified, recipes in this book serve four people.

CREMA DI ZUCCA

Cream of Squash

14 oz. squash, cut in large pieces
1 medium potato, cut in large pieces
2 small leeks, chopped
1 1/2 oz. butter, or 4 tablespoons pure olive oil

1 vegetable bouillon cube
1/2 cup cream (warm)
1/2 cup fresh parsley, chopped
Croutons, or 4-6 oz. cooked rice (optional)

1. Place potato, squash and leeks into a large Dutch oven casserole, add butter and parsley. Sauté over moderate heat for 10 minutes, stirring as needed. Do not brown vegetables.

2. Add 4 1/4 cups warm water. Add bouillon cube; bring to a boil, then lower heat and cook for 20-30 minutes.

3. Process in blender.

4. Return to casserole, add cream.

5. Taste for seasoning. Serve with croutons, or rice (optional).

CREMA DI PATATE E PORRI
Cream of Potato and Leek

2 large russet potatoes
2 or 3 leeks
1 vegetable bouillon cube
1 teaspoon fresh
   parsley, minced

1/4 cup cream,
   or 1/2 cup milk
Sea salt
4-5 tablespoons
   croutons (optional)

1. Peel and cut potatoes and leeks in medium pieces.

2. Cook vegetables in 4 cups of water for 20-30 minutes, add bouillon cube and parsley.

3. Process in blender; add enough cream or milk to obtain a medium thick consistency.

4. Place ingredients into saucepan, heat slightly.

5. Taste for seasoning. Serve with croutons (optional).

VARIATIONS:
a) Add parsley after cooking.
b) Garnish with paprika.
c) Season with grated lemon zest (do not grate the white inner layer).

CREMA DI LATTUGHE

Cream of Lettuce

4 large heads of lettuce	2 vegetable bouillons
1 large onion, sliced	4 cups water
1/2 oz. butter, or	6 tablespoons cream
2 tablespoons pure olive oil	1 tablespoon freshly
1 tablespoon flour	grated Parmigiano

1. Clean lettuce; cut into four parts, wash and drain well.

2. In large saucepan, melt butter over low heat, add onion and lettuce; cook 10 minutes over low heat.

3. Sprinkle with flour, blend well; cover with water; add bouillon; raise heat and cook until creamy.

4. Process in blender; return to pot and warm as needed.

5. Before serving, beat cream with Parmigiano. Pour over vegetables, stirring briskly 2-3 minutes.

6. Taste for seasoning. Serve with croutons (optional).

CREMA DI ASPARAGI (1)

Cream of Asparagus (1)

3 oz. butter, or 5 tablespoons
    pure olive oil
1/4 cup flour
4 cups milk
1 cup cream

3 tablespoons freshly
    grated Parmigiano
1 pound asparagus tips
    cooked in salted water
Sea salt

1. Melt butter in a saucepan over medium heat; add flour, cook a few minutes stirring constantly (do not brown flour).

2. Slowly add milk, stirring constantly until mixture reaches the consistency of a cream. Continue cooking 10-15 minutes, stirring occasionally.

3. Add asparagus, blend, heat slightly. Stir in cream and Parmigiano. Stir and cook 2 minutes; (do not boil!). Taste for seasoning.

VARIATIONS:
    Garnish with:
    a) small squares of potatoes, fried;
    b) croutons;
    c) small squares of carrots, cooked just until tender, then sauté in butter;
    d) young peas, cooked.

CREMA DI ASPARAGI (2)

Cream of Asparagus (2)

1 pound asparagus	1 cup cream
2 oz. butter, or 3 tablespoons pure olive oil	2 tablespoons freshly grated Parmigiano
1/4 cup flour	Sea salt
16 oz. vegetable bouillon	Croutons (optional)

1. Cut asparagus in small pieces, wash. Cook in boiling salted water for 15 minutes.

2. With butter, flour and bouillon make a medium sauce; add asparagus. Cook 15 minutes over low heat, stirring as needed.

3. Mix cream and Parmigiano; stir into soup, but do not boil.

4. Taste for seasoning. Serve with croutons (optional).

VARIATIONS:

Use the same procedure for:

a) Cream of cauliflower, adding a pinch of nutmeg.

b) Cream of spinach, seasoned with nutmeg, ginger, zest of 1 lemon.

c) Cream of leek.

d) Cream of peas.

e) Cream of onions: cook over very low heat (do not brown). Use 2 large onions, sliced, and saute in butter. When transparent, add flour and proceed as indicated for the cream of asparagus.

CREMA FREDDA DI CETRIOLI

Cold Cream of Cucumbers

1 1/2 oz. butter, or
    4 tablespoons pure olive oil
1/4 cup flour
2 large cucumbers
1 medium onion

2 cups prepared
    vegetable bouillon
1 cup yogurt
Sea salt

1. Peel cucumbers and onions, cut them into large pieces; boil 15-20 minutes in vegetable bouillon. Remove vegetables, mash and return to bouillon.

2. In a small saucepan, melt butter over low heat; add flour; stirring constantly, cook 2 minutes, but do not brown.

3. Slowly, pour bouillon into saucepan; add yogurt.

4. Bring to a boil, stirring constantly. Reduce heat to very low and cook 15 minutes, stirring as needed.

5. Taste for seasoning. Chill; serve very cold.

CREMA DI ZUCCA E CIPOLLE, DI ANTONELLA

Cream of Squash and Onion, Antonella's Recipe

Serves 6

1 1/2 pound squash (any type)
3/4 pound onion
4 cups vegetable bouillon
16 oz. red wine
1 large bay leaf
Pure olive oil

Parmigiano cheese
Nutmeg
Fresh parsley, minced
Sea salt
Black pepper
Croutons

1. Cut squash and onion in small squares. Heat oil; sauté vegetables with bay leaf; add salt, pepper.

2. Prepare vegetable bouillon with red wine.

3. Combine bouillon, squash and onion mixture; boil for 45 minutes.

4. Remove bay leaf. Cool.

5. Process ingredients in blender.

6. Reheat; season with Parmigiano and nutmeg.

Taste for seasoning. Serve with croutons.

CREMA DI MELANZANE, DI ANTONELLA

Cream of Eggplant, Antonella's Recipe   *Serves 8*

Skin of 4 large eggplants
1/2 onion
8 1/2 cups vegetable bouillon
8 oz. Porto wine
Pure olive oil

1 teaspoon butter
Nutmeg
Fresh parsley, minced
Croutons

1. Cut eggplant skin and onion in medium pieces; sauté in oil; add salt.

2. Prepare vegetable bouillon with Porto wine. Add to eggplant.

3. Cook for 45 minutes over medium heat.

4. Process ingredients in blender. Heat mixture slightly. Add butter, parsley and nutmeg.

Taste for seasoning. Serve with croutons.

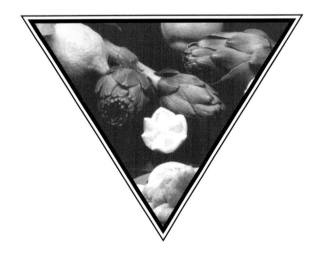

CREMA DI POMODORO

Cream of Tomato

4 tablespoons Italian
   tomato paste (Pomi brand)
1 onion, cut in quarters
1 stalk celery, cut in large pieces
1 carrot, cut in large pieces
4 cups vegetable bouillon
1 tablespoon flour

1 teaspoon fresh
   parsley, minced
1 teaspoon butter, or
   2 teaspoons pure olive oil
Whipping cream, unsweetened
Croutons

1. In a medium saucepan, combine onion, celery and carrot. Cover with vegetable bouillon and cook over medium high heat until vegetables are tender. Strain, but save liquid. Process vegetables in blender.

2. Return to saucepan; add butter and vegetable liquid. Sprinkle with flour, stir well. Add vegetables; stir well.

3. Dissolve tomato paste in a little water; add to vegetable cream; boil 10 minutes or until cream thickens.

4. Taste for seasoning. Serve very hot with croutons and whipping cream on the side.

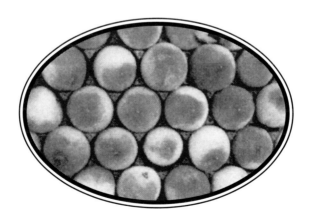

FLORENCE (Tuscany): Detail of the Cathedral "Santa Maria del Fiore" and Giotto's Campanile (bell-tower). The Dome of the cathedral was designed by Brunelleschi in 1418. It represents the symbolic birth of the Renaissance in Florence. The precious Campanile was designed in 1334 by Giotto when he was 73 years old. The tower is covered in colored marble and adorned with bas-relifs which are unique in Italy.

Florence was founded in the 1st century AD by the Romans who named her Fiorenza. The dialect of Tuscany assumed linguistic supremacy by the political importance of its principal city, Florence, and above all by the authority of the 13th century Florentine writers Dante, Petrarca and Boccaccio. Eventually, the Tuscan dialect became the official language of Italy.

Food and Wines. Florence has succeeded in conferring refinement and subtly on the most traditional and ordinary dishes. Basic ingredients of this delectable cuisine are olive oil and the excellent Chianti wine. Specialties are: fagioli all'uccelletto cooked with sage, garlic and tomato; beans boiled in a flask to keep all their flavor and dressed with olive oil, salt and pepper; minestrone di fagioli, a tasty bean soup seasoned with tomato and celery; tortino di carciofi, artichoke fried together with beaten eggs and seasoning.

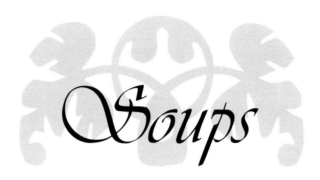

Soups

*Unless otherwise specified,
recipes in this book serve four people.*

STRACCIATELLE

Flakes of Eggs and Cheese

2 eggs

2 tablespoons
   freshly grated Parmigiano

2 teaspoons fresh parsley,
   chopped

4 cups vegetable bouillon

Pinch of nutmeg

Sea salt

1. Whisk eggs until just blended; mix in Parmigiano, parsley, nutmeg and a pinch of salt.

2. Prepare bouillon in a saucepan. Add egg mixture, stirring gently and constantly with a whisk.

3. Simmer while stirring 2-3 minutes. (Egg and cheese mixture will form tiny flakes in stock.)

4. Taste for seasoning. Serve at once.

ZUPPA PAVESE

Soup of Poached Eggs

4 eggs, very fresh (do not use substitute product)
4 slices Italian bread, 1/2 inch thick
4 tablespoons butter

4 cups vegetable bouillon
2 tablespoons grated Parmigiano
Black pepper

1. In a heavy skillet, melt butter over moderately low heat; add bread, turning frequently 4-5 minutes, or until bread is golden brown on both sides.

2. Prepare vegetable bouillon.

3. Place bread slices in individual soup bowls. Sprinkle with cheese.

4. Break 1 egg over each slice; season with black pepper; immediately pour hot bouillon over eggs.

5. Place in hot oven until eggs are cooked. Serve at once.

MINESTRONE ALLA FIORENTINA
Florentine Vegetable Soup

6 tablespoons pure olive oil

1 medium onion, coarsely cut

1 heart of celery, sliced

1 leek, thinly sliced

1/2 cup new potatoes,
   cut into small squares

1/2 cup carrots, sliced

1/2 cup zucchini, sliced

1/2 cup fresh beans
   (or dry, cooked)

1 cabbage, cut into thin slices

2 cups canned Italian tomatoes,
   chopped

1/2 cup fresh spinach

1/2 cup greens

1/2 cup tips of asparagus

1/2 cup peas

1/4 cup dry white beans

1/4 cup squash, diced

Sea salt

Black pepper

4 cups vegetable bouillon

3 cloves garlic, minced

1 teaspoon fresh parsley, minced

1 teaspoon fresh
   Italian basil, minced

1 bay leaf

2 cups cream

Freshly grated
   Parmigiano (optional)

1. In a large soup kettle, heat oil over medium heat; add onion and leek and sauté until they are soft and transparent, but not brown.

2. Add vegetables and beans, stir well to blend with oil (3-4 minutes). Add garlic and herbs, bay leaf and tomato. Stir well, cover, and steam 10 minutes.

3. Add bouillon to vegetables; add pepper and stir. Cover and cook 40 minutes over medium low heat.

4. When minestrone is almost done, add cream (do not boil!); blend well. Remove bay leaf. Taste for seasoning; serve hot.

NOTE:
   a) This dish is delicious without Parmigiano. I suggest you serve the cheese on the side.
   b) You can purée half the quantity of minestrone in a blender to make an excellent vegetable cream.

MINESTRA DI FINTA TAPIOCA

Imitation Tapioca Soup

5 cups vegetable bouillon
1 clove garlic, slightly crushed
1 bay leaf
3-4 large new potatoes,
   cut in half
1 egg yolk

2 tablespoons pure olive oil
1 tablespoon freshly
   grated Parmigiano
Sea salt
Black pepper

1. Prepare bouillon, add garlic and bay leaf. Bring to a boil; remove garlic.

2. Add potatoes, salt and pepper. Cook 10 minutes.

3. In soup bowl, whisk egg, Parmigiano and butter.

4. Pour hot bouillon over egg mixture. Taste for seasoning. Remove bay leaf. Serve at once.

ZUPPA DI SPINACI

Spinach Soup

14 oz. fresh spinach
1/2 onion, chopped
Fresh parsley, chopped
1 stalk celery, chopped
1 carrot, chopped
Pure olive oil

1-2 teaspoons Italian
   tomato sauce (Pomi brand)
2 vegetable bouillon cubes
4 tablespoons rice
1 tablespoon freshly
   grated Parmigiano

1. Sauté chopped onion, parsley, celery and carrot in hot oil.

2. Add spinach and tomato sauce. Cook 10 minutes over medium heat.

3. Purée through a sieve. Pour mixture back into saucepan; add enough water to make a regular soup consistency; add vegetable bouillon cubes. Bring to a boil; add rice; cook until "al dente."

4. Taste for seasoning. Stir in Parmigiano. Serve at once.

ZUPPA DI CIPOLLE
Onion Soup

4 large onions, thinly sliced
3 tablespoons pure olive oil
6 cups vegetable bouillon
12 thin small-size slices
   French bread
4 oz. Gruviera cheese

3 tablespoons Cognac
1 teaspoon sugar (scant)
Black pepper
1 tablespoon flour

1. In a heavy skillet, heat oil; add onions and sugar. Cover, cook over very low heat, stirring often.

2. When onions are slightly golden brown, sprinkle with flour; stir gently.

3. Pour in warm vegetable bouillon; bring to a boil.

4. Lower heat; simmer 20-30 minutes.

5. Meanwhile, toast bread slices.

6. When ready to serve, add Cognac and black pepper to soup.

7. Place 3 slices of bread into bottom of individual soup bowls; cover them with thin slices of Gruviera cheese. Pour the hot onion soup over bread.

Taste for seasoning. Serve at once.

ZUPPA DI CIPOLLE ALL'ITALIANA

Onion Soup Italian Style

4 large onions, thinly sliced
2 oz. butter, or 3 tablespoons
   pure olive oil
6 cups vegetable bouillon
12 thin small-size slices
   French bread
5 oz. Gorgonzola cheese

2 oz. freshly grated Parmigiano
2 tablespoons Cognac
Black pepper
Nutmeg
Sea salt

Prepare steps 1 through 6, as in previous recipe.

7. Place 3 bread slices in bottom of individual terra-cotta bowls. Place small pieces of Gorgonzola over bread; alternate bread and cheese.

8. Pour onion soup into individual bowls; sprinkle with Parmigiano.

9. Place in medium oven until cheese forms a crust. Serve at once.

ZUPPA DI FAGIOLI ALLA FIORENTINA
White Beans with Pasta

Serves 4 to 6

1 cup dry white beans
8 to 10 cups water
1/2 cup finely chopped onion
1/4 cup finely chopped celery
2 finely chopped garlic cloves
2 tablespoons pure olive oil
3 vegetable bouillon cubes

1/2 cup conchigliette; or thin
   spaghetti, cut into
   1-inch pieces
Freshly ground black pepper
Freshly grated
   Parmigiano cheese

1. In a 4 quart saucepan, bring beans and 8 cups water to a boil over high heat; boil 2 minutes.

2. Remove from heat; let beans soak 1 hour.

3. Drain beans and save liquid. To this liquid, add fresh cold water to make 8 cups.

4. Chop onions, celery and garlic into small pieces.

5. In a large Dutch oven, heat olive oil, stir in onions and celery; cook 10 minutes stirring frequently until lightly colored.

6. Add beans, water and bouillon cubes; season with pepper.

7. Bring to a boil, reduce heat and simmer, partially covered, 1 to 1 1/2 hours.

8. With a slotted spoon, remove half the beans and purée through a sieve; return to soup. Simmer over low heat 2 minutes, stirring constantly.

9. Add pasta and simmer until "al dente."

10. Taste for seasoning. Serve with sprinkled Parmigiano.

ZUPPA DI ZUCCA
Squash Soup

14 oz. squash (any type),
    cut into medium pieces
1 medium new potato,
    cut into medium pieces
1 medium zucchini,
    cut into medium pieces

2 small leeks, chopped
    into medium pieces
2 tablespoons pure olive oil
3 vegetable bouillon cubes
1/2 cup cream
1/2 cup fresh parsley, chopped

1. Place vegetables into a large saucepan, add oil and parsley. Sauté 10 minutes over moderate heat until they are well coated with oil; stir frequently. Do not brown vegetables.

2. Add 4 1/4 cups of warm water and bouillon cubes; bring to a boil; lower heat and cook 20-30 minutes.

3. Turn heat off; add cream; stir gently.

Taste for seasoning. Serve at once.

VERONA (*Veneto*): *The Roman Theater, called "the Arena Minor." Well-positioned against a hill, it is splendidly open to the views of the river and the city. The construction of the theater dates to the Augustan era, circa the second half of the 1st century BC. In this theater, every summer, is held the Shakespearean Festival.*

The region is famous for the best Italian wine, "Soave."

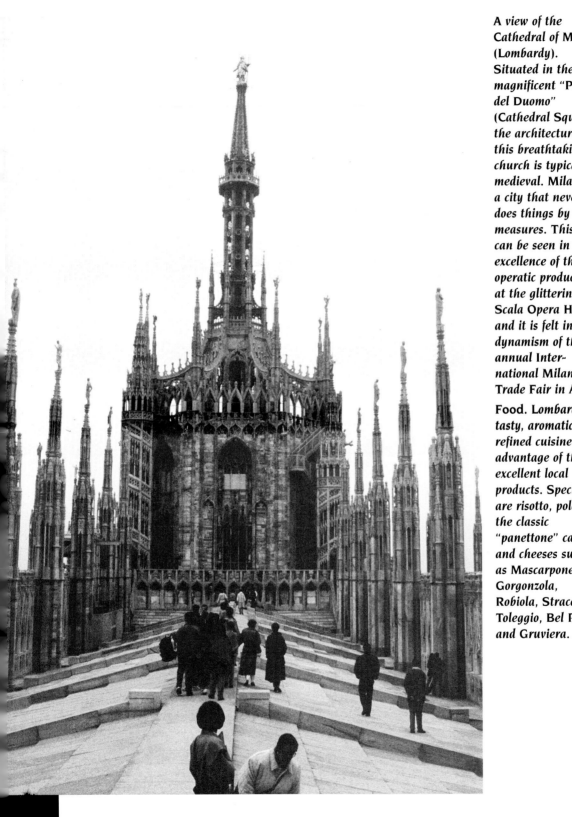

A view of the Cathedral of MILAN (Lombardy). Situated in the magnificent "Piazza del Duomo" (Cathedral Square), the architecture of this breathtaking church is typically medieval. Milan is a city that never does things by half measures. This can be seen in the excellence of the operatic productions at the glittering La Scala Opera House, and it is felt in the dynamism of the annual International Milan Trade Fair in April.

Food. Lombardy's tasty, aromatic and refined cuisine takes advantage of the excellent local products. Specialties are risotto, polenta, the classic "panettone" cake, and cheeses such as Mascarpone, Gorgonzola, Robiola, Stracchino, Toleggio, Bel Paese and Gruviera.

Rice

*Among the best Italian rice, I suggest Vialone or Arborio -
both tolerate cooking temperature well and they can be used
in all rice recipes. I have described the proper way
to prepare rice in "Simple Recipes (1) and (2)" below.*

*Unless otherwise specified,
recipes in this book serve four people.*

RISOTTO SEMPLICE (1)

Simple Recipe (1)

1 cup Italian rice
4 cups good vegetable
  bouillon (set aside 1 cup)

1/2 teaspoon butter, or
  1 tablespoon pure olive oil
Freshly grated Parmigiano

1. Bring to a boil 3 cups of bouillon. Add rice and cook uncovered over high heat for 15 minutes, stirring frequently.

2. Add reserved (warm) bouillon, as needed. Continue cooking, covered, until rice is almost done. Blend in butter and Parmigiano.

Taste for seasoning. Let stand 3-5 minutes before serving.

RISOTTO SEMPLICE (2)

Simple Recipe (2)

Ingredients as above recipe, but double the quantity of butter or oil.

1. In a saucepan, melt 1/2 teaspoon butter or pure olive oil. Add rice and sauté 2 minutes over moderate heat.

2. Add 3 cups of good, warm vegetable bouillon. Cook uncovered over high heat, stirring occasionally. Add reserved bouillon as needed.

3. Lower heat to a simmer until rice is almost done. Stir in remaining butter and Parmigiano.

Taste for seasoning. Let stand for 3-5 minutes before serving.

RISOTTO AL POMODORO

Rice with Tomatoes

1 cup Italian rice	1 teaspoon butter, or
2 tablespoons tomato sauce	1 tablespoon pure olive oil
(see pages 71, 72)	Freshly grated Parmigiano

1. Bring 4 cups of water to a boil. Add rice, stirring frequently; add warm water as needed.

2. Cook 10 minutes; add tomato sauce and cook until rice is almost done.

3. Lower heat to very low. Blend in butter and Parmigiano.

Taste for seasoning. Let stand 3-5 minutes before serving.

RISI E BISI
Braised Rice and Peas

1 cup Italian rice

1 cup peas

4 tablespoons butter, or
  5 tablespoons pure olive oil

1 small onion, minced

2 cups vegetable bouillon

2 tablespoons fresh
  parsley, minced

Sea salt

White pepper

1. In a saucepan, melt butter; add onion and sauté until transparent, but not brown. Add parsley, peas and rice. Cook 2 minutes.

2. Add enough bouillon to cover ingredients. Cook until liquid is absorbed. Add more bouillon and cook until peas are tender. Blend in white pepper.

Taste for seasoning. Serve at once.

RISOTTO CON FUNGHI
Rice with Mushrooms

Prepare a Simple Rice (2) - see page 46; except:

1. First, sauté 1/2 small minced onion in oil. When onion is golden, add 1 cup fresh sliced mushrooms. I prefer dried Shiitake mushrooms (Champignon Séchè).

2. Add rice and a small cup of dry white wine. Cook until liquid is completely absorbed. Then proceed to add bouillon as needed until rice is "al dente."

Taste for seasoning. Serve at once.

RISO PILAF

Classic Rice

1 cup Italian rice
4 oz. butter
1 tablespoon pure olive oil
1 onion, minced

4 cups vegetable bouillon
Sea salt
Pepper (optional)

1. In an oven-proof casserole, sauté onion in 3 oz. butter and 1 tablespoon olive oil.

2. Add rice; stir 2-3 minutes, or until rice glistens with butter and oil.

3. Add 4 cups of bouillon (3 times the volume of rice). Bring to a boil.

4. Place in oven at moderate heat for 15-20 minutes.

5. Remove from oven when rice is just done; blend in remaining butter with a fork.

Taste for seasoning. Serve at once.

RISO IN CAGNONE

Zesty Rice

1 cup Italian rice
4 oz. butter

4 oz. freshly grated Parmigiano
3 cloves garlic, crushed
1 sprig fresh sage

1. Cook rice in 3 to 4 cups of boiling water; drain when almost done. Place into serving dish. Sprinkle with Parmigiano.

2. Over low heat, sauté sage, garlic and butter until butter is slightly brown. Remove sage and garlic. Pour butter over rice, completely covering the cheese.

3. Carefully blend the butter and cheese into rice. Serve at once.

RISOTTO ALLA MILANESE

Rice and Saffron

1 cup Italian rice
4 oz. butter, or
   5 tablespoons pure olive oil
4 1/4 cups very good
   vegetable bouillon
1/2 cup dry Marsala,
   or 1 cup dry white wine

1 medium onion, minced
1/2 teaspoon saffron
2 oz. freshly
   grated Parmigiano
Sea salt (optional)

1. Melt 2 oz. butter in a saucepan, add onion and sauté on low heat until transparent.

2. Add rice and stir until it glistens with butter (1-2 minutes). Add Marsala; increase heat and reduce the liquid to half.

3. Cover rice with 4 cups of warm bouillon; add saffron dissolved in 1 tablespoon of cold bouillon. Cook over low heat, stirring frequently; add warm bouillon as needed.

4. Remove from heat when rice is barely done. Add Parmigiano and butter, stir well. Let stand 3-5 minutes. Taste for seasoning. Serve at once.

RISO AL LIMONE
Rice with Lemon

6 qts. water	3 eggs, or substitute product
1 cup Italian rice	1 cup freshly
Sea salt	grated Parmigiano
2 tablespoons butter, or	4 teaspoons lemon juice
3 tablespoons pure olive oil	

1. In a large kettle, bring water and salt to a boil over high heat. Add rice in a slow steam (do not let water stop boiling). Stir once or twice.

2. Reduce to moderate heat and boil uncovered and undisturbed for about 15 minutes, or until tender. Do not stir. Drain rice in a large colander.

3. Over low heat, melt butter in a 1-qt. flame-proof casserole and immediately add hot drained rice.

4. In a bowl, beat eggs, cheese and lemon juice with a fork until well combined.

5. Stir this mixture into rice and cook over low heat, stirring gently with a fork 3-4 minutes.

Taste for seasoning. Serve at once while rice is still creamy.

VENICE (Veneto): The Historical Regatta down the Grand Canal. In September, gondole and other craft are decorated for this event. Venice is built on a lagoon containing more than 118 islands and divided by 160 canals joined by 400 bridges. The city was founded in the 7th century AD during the Longobardi invasions when the people of the region took refuge in the islands around the coast of the peninsula. The Grand Canal is called the most beautiful "street" of the world for its splendid palaces.

Food and Wines. Venetian cooking is straightforward and homely. Simple dishes use onions, greens and vegetables. Well-known dishes are "risi and bisi" (rice and peas), beans noodle soup, polenta, radicchio. The best wine of this region is Valpolicella.

The unparalleled setting of Piazza di Spagna with the stairway of Trinita` dei Monti designed by Michelangelo. (Rome). This square is the best -known of all Rome's "piazze." Spanish steps are ablaze with flowers in Spring.

Food and wines. The cuisine of Rome involves healthy portions and well-seasoned, tasty, and hearty dishes which include: carciofi alla romana, artichokes stuffed with garlic and mint and cooked with plenty of oil over low heat; fungo arrosto, tasty mushrooms seasoned with garlic, olive oil and parsley, and roasted; gnocchi served with butter and grated cheese; maccheroni alla ricotta, maccheroni served with a sauce made of cottage cheese, salted and peppered; spaghetti al cacio e pepe, spaghetti served with "pecorino" (a very strong goat's cheese) and pepper. The best wines are: Frascati, Colli Albani, Est!Est!Est!

Gnocchi and Polenta

Unless otherwise specified,
recipes in this book serve four people.

GNOCCHI VERDI

Spinach Dumplings

8 tablespoons butter	2 eggs, lightly beaten
2 ten-ounce packages frozen chopped spinach, thoroughly defrosted, squeezed completely dry, and chopped very fine (about 1 1/2 cups), or 1 1/2 pounds fresh spinach, cooked, squeezed and chopped	6 tablespoons flour
	3/4 cup freshly grated Parmigiano
	1/2 teaspoon Sea salt
	1/2 teaspoon freshly ground black pepper
	Pinch of ground nutmeg
3/4 cup Ricotta cheese	6 to 8 qts. water

1. In an 8-to-10 inch enameled or stainless-steel skillet, melt 4 tablespoons butter over moderate heat. Add chopped fresh or frozen spinach and cook, stirring constantly, 2-3 minutes, or until almost all moisture has boiled away and spinach begins to stick lightly to the skillet. Add 3/4 cup Ricotta and cook, stirring, 3-4 minutes longer.

2. With a rubber spatula, transfer entire contents of skillet to a large mixing bowl and stir in 2 lightly beaten eggs, 6 tablespoons of flour, 1/4 cup of grated Parmigiano, 1/2 teaspoon salt, pepper and nutmeg. Place in refrigerator for 30 minutes to 1 hour, or until Gnocchi mixture is quite firm.

3. Bring 6 to 8 qts. water and 1 tablespoon salt to a simmer over moderate heat, in a large soup pot or saucepan. Flour your hands lightly and form small balls (about 1 1/2 inch in diameter) of chilled Gnocchi mixture. Gently drop balls into simmering water and cook uncovered 5 to 8 minutes, or until they puff slightly and are somewhat firm to the touch. With a slotted spoon, lift Gnocchi out of water and set aside on a towel to drain.

4. Preheat broiler. Pour 2 tablespoons melted butter into a shallow 8 by 12 inch flameproof dish and swirl butter around until bottom of dish glistens. Arrange Gnocchi in the dish in a single layer about 1/4-inch apart; dribble remaining 2 tablespoons melted butter over them. Sprinkle Gnocchi with remaining 1/2 cup grated Parmigiano. Place under broiler 3 inches from heat for 3 minutes, or until cheese melts.

Serve Gnocchi at once, directly from the baking dish. Serve additional grated cheese separately, if you wish.

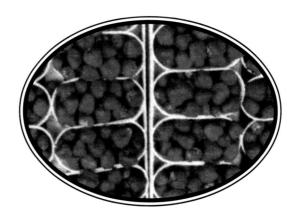

GNOCCHI ALLA ROMANA

Semolina Cakes with Butter and Cheese   *Serves 4 to 6*

3 cups milk
1 1/2 teaspoons salt
Pinch of ground nutmeg
Freshly ground black pepper
3/4 cup semolina or flour

2 eggs (slightly beaten)
1 cup freshly
   grated Parmigiano
4 tablespoons butter, melted

1. Butter a large baking sheet and set it aside. In a heavy 2 to 3 quart saucepan, bring milk, nutmeg and a few grindings of pepper to a boil over medium heat. Slowly pour the semolina into boiling milk, making sure boiling never stops. Stir constantly with a wooden spoon until semolina is thick. Remove pan from the heat.

2. Add 3/4 cup Parmigiano to eggs and blend this mixture into the semolina.

3. Dip a metal spatula or knife in hot water, then smooth and spread semolina onto the baking sheet, about 1/4 inch thick. Refrigerate for at least an hour, or until semolina is firm.

4. Preheat oven to 400 degrees; grease a deep bake-and-serve dish (8-9 inches wide). With a biscuit cutter, or a sharp knife, cut semolina into small circles or triangles. Place Gnocchi in the baking dish, add melted butter and sprinkle with the remaining 1/4 cup of Parmigiano cheese.

5. Bake Gnocchi on middle shelf of medium heat oven for 15 minutes, or until they are crisp and golden. If you prefer them browned, place dish under hot broiler for 30 seconds.

Serve immediately.

POLENTA

Corn-Meal Porridge

Serves 6

6 cups water
2 teaspoons salt

**1 1/2 cups finely
ground Polenta**

1. In a heavy 3 to 4 qt saucepan, bring water and salt to a boil over high heat. Slowly pour uncooked Polenta into boiling water, making sure boiling never stops. Stir constantly to keep mixture smooth.

2. Reduce heat and simmer Polenta, stirring frequently 20 to 30 minutes, or until it is so thick that a spoon stands unsupported in the middle of the pan. Remove from heat.

***Polenta can be served with the following sauces*:**
- Bread and Cheese (see page 16.)
- Fried Polenta (see below)
- Polenta with Cream Sauce and Mushrooms (see page 57)
- Tomato Sauce (see page 71, 72)

POLENTA FRITTA

Fried Polenta

1. Prepare the Polenta porridge as in the above recipe. Refrigerate for about 2 hours. Cut Polenta into rectangular slices.

2. Fry Polenta in plenty of hot pure olive oil.

3. Serve with soft, fat cheese. (see "Cheeses of Italy," pages xvii, xviii.)

POLENTA PASTICCIATA
Polenta with Cream Sauce and Mushrooms

Prepare the Polenta porridge (see page 56).

BESCIAMELLA FOR POLENTA

**5 tablespoons butter,
or 6 tablespoons
pure olive oil
5 tablespoons flour
2 cups milk
1/2 cup heavy cream
Pinch of ground nutmeg
1 teaspoon Sea salt**

**Pepper
3/4 cup freshly
grated Parmigiano
3/4 pound fresh mushrooms,
thinly sliced. I prefer dried
Shiitake mushrooms
(Champignon Séchè).**

1. In a heavy 2 to 3 qt. saucepan, melt 3 tablespoons of butter over medium heat and stir in flour. Remove pan from heat and add milk and cream, beating with a wire whisk until flour is partially blended.

2. Return pan to high heat and cook, stirring constantly with a whisk until sauce comes to a boil and is thick and smooth. Reduce heat and simmer, still stirring, 2-3 minutes. Remove pan from heat and stir in nutmeg, salt and pepper. Then add 1/2 cup grated Parmigiano; set pan aside.

3. Melt 2 tablespoons butter in a heavy 8 to 10 inch skillet. Add mushrooms, tossing constantly with a spoon, for 3-4 minutes, or until they glisten with butter and are slightly colored.

4. Preheat oven to 375 degrees. Cut Polenta in half crosswise and lay one half in buttered shallow 8 by 8 inch bake-and-serve dish. Spread half the mushrooms over Polenta and spoon half Besciamella on them. Place second half Polenta on top and spread it with the rest of the mushrooms and Besciamella. Sprinkle with remaining 1/4 cup Parmigiano.

5. Bake on middle shelf of oven for 25-30 minutes, or until cheese and sauce are browned and bubbling. Carefully cut into squares. Serve at once.

SIENA (Tuscany): A view of Piazza del Campo and Tower of Mangia. The city was founded by the Romans in the 1st century BC who named her Sena Julia. Twice a year, on the 2nd of July and on the 16th August, the Sienese hold the "Palio" with splendid costumes of the 14th century. The Palio is a long silk banner painted with a religious theme and awarded to the contrada whose horse wins the often violent three-lap race. The Festa is held around the shell-shaped Piazza del Campo where tension mounts to an unbearable fever of excitement. When it is over, there is triumph and glory for the victorious contrada. Celebrations with traditional songs and feasts last for days and nights.

Food and wines. Siena is famous for the "Panforte" cake made of spices and almonds. The best wines are Montepulciano, Montalcino, Chianti. The production of olive oil is extensive.

Eggs and Frittate

Cook hard boiled eggs in salted boiling water for 7 or 8 minutes (no longer!).
Then, place eggs in a large bowl of cold water to stop the cooking time.
Cook frittate over high heat. When done, they must
be golden outside and soft inside.

*Unless otherwise specified,
recipes in this book serve four people.*

UOVA SODE RIPIENE
Stuffed Hard Boiled Eggs

1. Serve stuffed hard boiled eggs over a bed of lettuce, cut into strips, and dressed with pure olive oil, vinegar or lemon, salt and pepper.

2. Fill halved egg whites with:
   a) Mashed egg yolks, butter, minced herbs (basil, parsley, leek, a bit of garlic), lemon juice, and a few drops of tobasco.
   b) Mashed egg yolks, puree of peas, butter, Mayonnaise, fresh mint.

UOVA ALL'INDIANA
Hard Boiled Eggs with Apples

Mix cubes of hard boiled eggs with cubes of apples (sour types), Mayonnaise seasoned with lemon juice and diluted with milk or cream. Blend powdered curry into mixture; blend well. Taste for seasoning.

UOVA SODE AL CURRY
Hard Boiled Eggs with Curry

4 hard boiled eggs
1/2 teaspoon curry
4 tablespoons cream
8 almonds, minced
2 tablespoons butter, or
   3 tablespoons pure olive oil

1 tablespoon flour
8 oz. milk
Sea salt

1. Cut eggs in half lengthwise, remove yolks and place them in a bowl.

2. With 1 tablespoon butter, flour and 4 oz. of milk, prepare a firm Besciamella (see page 1). Place 3-4 tablespoons of mixture in the bowl with the yolks.

3. Over medium heat, dilute the remaining Besciamella with cream and remaining 4 oz. of milk. Remove from heat, salt and mix with curry.

4. Mash yolks with a fork, blend mixture with almonds. Fill egg whites with this mixture; place them into a pan, greased with melted butter.

5. Cover egg whites with Besciamella and curry mixture; place them in a medium hot oven for 5-10 minutes, or until they are golden crisp.

UOVA BARZOTTE

Soft Boiled Eggs

1. Reduce cooking time for boiled eggs from 8 to 6 minutes (see description for cooking hard boiled eggs, page 59). Place in cold water to stop cooking time. Carefully remove the shell.

2. To serve cold, cover eggs until ready to serve.

3. To serve warm, keep them in warm water (not too hot!).

Serve eggs with several sauces (see "Sauces" chapter, pages 1 to 12).

UOVA ALLA CANNELLA

Eggs with Cinnamon

Prepare Egg Barzotte (see above). Place them in a warm dish; cover with freshly grated Parmigiano, sprinkle with cinnamon; cover with very hot melted butter.

UOVA STRAPAZZATE
Scrambled Eggs

This recipe requires very low heat.

1. Use 2 eggs per person. Break eggs in a small bowl, add salt and pepper (optional). With a fork, break yolks and then beat them just enough to mix with egg whites.

2. Heat a small amount of butter or pure olive oil in a pan; over low heat, add eggs stirring constantly. Remove eggs from heat when they are very soft.

If you prefer, stir into eggs (at the end of cooking time):
   a) A small amount of liquid cream.
   b) A teaspoon fresh butter.
   c) A generous amount of cream and several drops Worcestershire sauce.
   d) Golden crisp croutons sautéed in butter.
   e) A small amount of tomato sauce (see pages 71, 72).

UOVA ALLO SHERRY
Eggs with Sherry

This recipe is delicious.

8 eggs
3 oz. butter
2 tablespoons dry Sherry

3 tablespoons freshly grated Gruviera cheese
Sea salt

1. In a bowl, combine eggs, Gruviera cheese, Sherry, salt (optional). Beat ingredients just enough to blend mixture.

2. In a skillet, melt 2 oz. butter; add eggs. Cook over low heat, stirring constantly, lifting the mixture from the bottom of pan.

3. Remove from heat while mixture is still creamy.

4. Add remaining butter, mix well. Complement dish with fresh crisp croutons, or toast cut into triangles. Serve immediately.

UOVA ALLA CREMA

Eggs with Cream and Curry

8 eggs
3 oz. butter, or 5 tablespoons
   pure olive oil
4 tablespoons cream,
   fresh or sour
2 teaspoons curry

3 chestnuts, shelled
1/2 teaspoons of ginger strips
   in syrup (ginger gives the
   dish an exotic taste)
Sea salt

1. Mix curry with cream; mixture must be smooth; add eggs and salt, stirring well.

2 and 3, follow as in "Eggs with Sherry" recipe, page 62.

4. Add butter, mixing until well blended.

5. Serve with decoration of shelled, quartered chestnuts and strips of ginger.

UOVA ALL'OREGANO

Eggs with Oregano

1. Over medium heat, melt 2 teaspoons of butter and sauté 1 or 2 cloves of garlic, mashed, for 1 minute.

2. Remove garlic; add 8 eggs; cook over medium heat until done; sprinkle with a pinch of oregano.

3. Place eggs on serving dish; sprinkle with plenty of freshly grated Parmigiano.

FRITTATA SEMPLICE
Simple Frittata

1. Beat 6 or 8 eggs (or substitute product) just enough to blend yolks and whites - no longer.
2. In a fry pan, heat pure olive oil on high heat until bubbling; add in eggs.
3. Stir briskly with a wooden spoon.
4. When the frittata is firm, shake the fry pan to loosen the contents from the bottom.
5. Place a dish over the pan and invert the frittata on to dish.
6. Pour a small amount of pure olive oil in the fry pan and heat.
7. Carefully, slide the uncooked side of the frittata into pan. Cook over high heat until done.

ADDITIONS TO SIMPLE FRITTATA.
Blend eggs with the following ingredients:
   a) 2 tablespoons freshly grated Parmigiano.
   b) 1 small boiled potato, cut into small cubes . Cook
       1/2 tablespoon of minced onion over low heat in
       1 or 2 tablespoons pure olive oil and mix with cubed potato.
   c) 1 tablespoon minced onion, uncooked, or cooked over low
       heat in a tablespoon pure olive oil. Add 1 tablespoon fresh,
       minced parsley or 1 tablespoon fresh basil, minced.
   d) Plenty of paprika and 1 tablespoon uncooked onion, minced.
   e) 1 tablespoon fresh parsley, minced, and 1 small potato, cut
       into squares and cooked in butter until golden brown.
   f) 1 small chopped onion and 1 chopped pepper cooked in
       3 tablespoons pure olive oil until tender (15 minutes). Do not
       brown!
The above "frittate," especially c, d, f, are very good when served cold.

FRITTATINE CON SPINACI

Small Frittate with Spinach

Serves 2

3 eggs
1 tablespoon freshly
grated Parmigiano
3 tablespoons spinach
sauteed in butter

2 tablespoons thick tomato
sauce (see pages 71, 72)
Pure olive oil
Sea salt, pepper

1. In a small bowl, beat eggs with Parmigiano, salt, pepper and 1 teaspoon water. Cook 4 small frittate. Place into individual dishes.

2. Fill frittate with very warm spinach sautéed in butter; garnish with warm tomato sauce.

TORTINO DI CARCIOFI

Baked Artichoke Heart Frittata

4 eggs
2 tablespoons pure olive oil
Sea salt

1 cup frozen artichoke hearts,
defrosted and cut
lengthwise into quarters

1. Preheat oven to 400 degrees. In a small bowl, beat eggs and a pinch of salt with a whisk or rotary beater until they are foamy and well combined. Set them aside.

2. Heat olive oil in 8 to 10 inch skillet. Drop in artichokes and cook over moderate heat, stirring frequently for 5 minutes, or until golden brown.

3. Spread artichokes over bottom of buttered 1-qt. bake-and-serve dish. Pour beaten eggs over them.

4. Bake in upper third of medium heat oven for 15 minutes, or until frittata is firm and knife inserted in its center comes out clean. Serve the "Tortino" at once.

NOTE:
In Italy, the "Tortino" is traditionally made with tiny artichokes. The whole artichokes are cleaned, trimmed and cooked in boiling water for about 15 minutes, or until tender, before they are sauteed.

FRITTATA ALLA SARDEGNOLA

Zucchini Frittata

3 cups water

1 cup diced unpeeled
   fresh zucchini

2 tablespoons fresh
   white bread crumbs

3 tablespoons milk

4 tablespoons freshly
   grated Parmigiano

1/4 teaspoon freshly
   grated lemon zest

Sea salt

Pinch sugar

4 eggs

2 tablespoons pure olive oil

1. Preheat broiler to highest setting. Over medium heat, bring water and salt to a bubbling boil in a small saucepan. Drop in diced zucchini and blanch 3 minutes. Drain thoroughly in large colander.

2. In a small mixing bowl, soak bread crumbs in milk 5 minutes. Stir in zucchini, grated Parmigiano, lemon zest, salt, sugar.

3. In another bowl, beat eggs with whisk or fork until just blended; then stir gently into bread-crumb-zucchini mixture.

4. Heat oil in a 10-inch skillet. Pour in egg-and-zucchini mixture and cook over medium heat 2 or 3 minutes, or until eggs are firm but still slightly moist.

5. Place skillet under broiler for 30 seconds to brown the top lightly. Slide frittata into serving dish and serve at once.

A *typical village in* **SARDINIA.**
*This island of fields, forests and
stones is gently surrounded by the
sea which gracefully illuminates
the coastline. From Alghero to the
Emerald Coast, the entire Sardinia*
*coast exists together united by
stones, yachts and the fishing
boats equipped with the "lampara"
(a lantern hung before the bow).
The island peaks, the tall
"faraglioni," stand as sentinels in*
*the sea to protect the cliffs, towers,
natural pinnacles, grottoes and a
whole constellation of smaller
islands.*

**Sardinia's best wines are Vernaccia
and Moscato del Campidano.**

POSITANO (Naples). The stunning blue shoreline of the Amalfi Gulf is magnificently arrayed with beaches and wild reefs, and vertical, polychrome villages that look like works of art. This is the place of emerald grottoes, little ports, inlets for underwater fishing, tiny pensions, pizza restaurants, boutiques and ceramic studios, terraced lemon groves, and small squares where one hears a mixture of many languages.

Food and wines. Specialties of the Campania region are: calzoni alla napoletana, dough containing mozzarella cheese and tomato, either fried in olive oil or baked; mozzarella in carrozza, a slice of fresh, sweet mozzarella cheese between two slices of bread, dipped in batter and fried in olive oil; spaghetti al pomodoro - this dish can be found all over Italy and in many other parts of the world, but its home is here. It is made of high quality wheat flour and cooked until "only just" done, (al dente), then served with a light sauce made of fresh tomatoes which have been cooked in olive oil with spices, often basil. The best wines are: white and red Capri, Lacrima Christi and Vesuvio.

Pasta and Sauces

Today, the supermarket offers a wide variety of pasta: spaghetti linguine, perciatelli, maccheroni, zite, wide lasagne, green lasagne, fusilli, farfalle, gnocchetti siciliani, conchigliette, tagliatelle, fettuccine, pappardelle. Many of these products are excellent, especially those imported from Italy. However, if you prefer "homemade" pasta, the following recipe explains how to make, by hand, the basic dough for egg noodles. Using this recipe, you can cut the dough into a variety of sizes and shapes to prepare cannelloni, tortellini, ravioli, tagliarini, fettuccine, tagliatelle and lasagne.

Unless otherwise specified, recipes in this book serve four people.

PASTA ALL'UOVO
Homemade Egg Noodles

Makes about 3/4 pound

1 1/2 cups unsifted
   all-purpose flour
1 egg
1 egg white

1 tablespoons pure olive oil
1 teaspoon Sea salt
A few drops water

Put the flour into a large mixing bowl or in a heap on a pastry board; make a well in the center of the flour; add the egg, egg white, oil and salt. Mix together with a fork or your fingers until dough can be gathered into a ball. Moisten any remaining dry bits of flour with drops of water and press them into the ball.

TO MAKE PASTA BY HAND:

1. Knead the dough on a floured board, working in a little extra flour if the dough seems sticky. After 10 minutes, the dough should be smooth, shiny and elastic. Wrap it in plastic wrap and let the dough rest at least 10 minutes before rolling it.

2. Divide dough into 2 balls. Place 1 ball on a floured board or pastry cloth and flatten it with the palm of your hand into a rectangle about 1 inch thick. Dust the top lightly with flour. Then, using a heavy rolling pin, start at one end of the rectangle and roll it lengthwise away from yourself to within an inch or so of the farthest edge. Turn dough crosswise and roll across its width. Repeat, turning and rolling the dough, until it is paper thin. If at any time the dough begins to sticks, lift it carefully and sprinkle more flour under it.

3. To make tagliarini, fettuccine, tagliatelle and lasagne, dust rolled dough lightly with flour and let it rest for about 10 minutes. Then, gently roll dough into jelly-roll shape.

4. With a long sharp knife, slice the roll crosswise into even strips - 1/8 inch wide for tagliarini, 1/4 inch wide for fettuccine or tagliatelle, 1 1/2 to 2 inches wide for lasagne. Unroll the strips and set them aside on wax paper. In the same fashion, roll, shape and slice the second half of dough.

5. Homemade egg noodles may be covered tightly with plastic wrap and kept in the refrigerator for as long as 24 hours.

COOKING THE PASTA

All kinds of pasta are cooked in the same way:

1. In a large pot, bring 4 to 5 quarts of water to a bubbling boil, add a scant amount of Sea salt.

2. Drop the pasta slowly and in small portions into boiling water, stirring gently with a wooden fork for a few minutes to prevent the strands from sticking to one another or to the bottom of the pot. Boil over high heat, stirring occasionally, until the pasta is just tender. Test it by tasting: pasta should be soft but "al dente" (slightly resistant to the bite).

3. Drain immediately into a colander; lift the strands with 2 forks to make sure it is thoroughly drained. Transfer pasta at once to a hot serving bowl.

4. To obtain a thorough coating of the pasta, first sprinkle with freshly grated imported cheese, then add the sauce; toss well and serve at once.

NOTE:
Do not rinse the cooked pasta unless you are preparing cannelloni or lasagne. In this case, they must be cooked "al dente;" rinsed briefly with cold water to stop cooking time; then, dried and stuffed or baked.

Sauces for Pasta

All types of pasta can be seasoned with pure olive oil,
freshly grated Parmigiano and tomato sauce. I have selected several
recipes of tomato sauces, each having a different flavor.
Place the leftover sauce in a glass container, cover it with a thin coat of pure
olive oil; refrigerate for no more than a week.

SALSA DI POMODORO (1)

Tomato Sauce (1)

This is the tomato recipe I prefer because it is cooked with no fats and is, therefore, healthier.

1 18-ounce can	**1-2 garlic cloves**
Italian tomatoes	**1 tablespoon fresh parsley**
1 medium onion,	**2-3 leaves fresh Italian basil**
cut into quarters	**Sea salt**

Combine all ingredients into a small saucepan (do not use enamel pan); bring to a boil. Lower the heat and continue cooking, covered, for 30 minutes. Process mixture in blender. If the sauce is too thin, reheat over medium heat to condense liquid.

SALSA DI POMODORO (2)

Tomato Sauce (2)

3 tablespoons pure olive oil
6-7 canned Italian tomatoes
1 medium onion, minced

Pinch of nutmeg
Sea salt

1. Over low heat, cook onion in oil until soft and transparent. Add tomatoes, drained and crushed with a fork. Cook uncovered over low heat 15 minutes to reduce liquid and thicken sauce.

2. Flavor with nutmeg. Taste for seasoning.

SALSA DI POMODORO (3)

Tomato Sauce (3)

1. Heat 3 tablespoons pure olive oil in a small frypan; sauté 1 tablespoon minced fresh Italian basil. Add 1 18-ounce can tomatoes (well drained and cut). Salt sparingly. Cook over low heat 5 minutes.

2. Remove sauce from heat and process in blender.

3. Season pasta with this sauce; add 2 tablespoons of pure olive oil and 1/2 cup freshly grated Parmigiano, or grated Pecorino, or Ricotta. Toss well.

QUICK TOMATO SAUCE

4 tablespoons pure olive oil
6-7 canned Italian tomatoes
1 bay leaf

Pinch of sugar
Worcestershire sauce
Sea salt

1. In a small saucepan, combine tomatoes (well drained and crushed with a fork), bay leaf, salt, sugar. Boil to reduce liquid over medium high heat; cook 10-15 minutes.

2. Remove from heat; add a few drops Worcestershire sauce.

3. Flavor pasta with this sauce, adding uncooked butter and freshly grated Parmigiano.

PESTO ALLA GENOVESE

Basil, Garlic and Cheese Sauce   *Makes about 1 1/2 to 2 cups*

2 cups fresh Italian basil leaves, stripped from their stems, coarsely minced and tightly packed

1 teaspoon salt

1/2 teaspoon freshly ground black pepper

1 to 2 teaspoons finely chopped garlic

2 tablespoons finely chopped pine nuts

1 to 1 1/2 cups pure olive oil

1/2 cup freshly grated imported Sardo or Romano or Parmigiano cheese

TO MAKE THE PESTO IN A BLENDER:

1. Combine basil, salt, pepper, garlic, pine nuts and 1 cup olive oil in blender jar. Process at high speed until ingredients are smooth, stopping blender every 5 or 6 seconds to push herbs down with a rubber spatula.

2. The sauce should be thin enough to run off the spatula easily. If it is too thick, blend in up to 1/2 cup extra olive oil. Transfer sauce to a bowl and stir in grated cheese.

NOTE:
   a) Generally, in Italy the pesto is thinned further by adding 1 to 2 tablespoons of the hot pasta water before mixing it with pasta.
   b) Never heat pesto. Serve it uncooked, at room temperature, or chilled.
   c) Mix the pesto with pasta off the heat. Serve immediately.
   d) Refrigerate or freeze any leftover pesto.

SALSA PIZZAIOLA

Tomato and Garlic Sauce

Makes about 3 cups

3 tablespoons pure olive oil
1 cup finely chopped onions
1 tablespoon finely chopped garlic
4 cups Italian or whole-pack tomatoes, coarsely chopped but not drained
1 six-ounce can Italian tomato paste (Pomi brand)

1 tablespoon dried oregano, crumbled
1 tablespoon finely cut fresh Italian basil
1 bay leaf
2 teaspoons sugar
1 1/2 teaspoon Sea salt
Freshly ground black pepper

1. In a 3 to 4 quart saucepan, heat 3 tablespoons olive oil and cook onions over medium heat, stirring frequently, 7-8 minutes. When onions are soft and transparent, add garlic and cook 1-2 minutes more, stirring constantly.

2. Stir in tomatoes and their liquid, tomato paste, oregano, basil, bay leaf, sugar, salt and pepper. Bring sauce to a boil, reduce heat to very low and simmer uncovered, stirring occasionally for 1 hour.

3. When done, the sauce should be thick and fairly smooth. Remove bay leaf.

Taste for seasoning. Serve with all types of pasta; also lasagne.

TORTELLINI ALLA CREMA

Tortellini with Cream

1. In a saucepan, cook the tortellini until just tender. Drain.

2. In another saucepan, heat cream (1 cup for 11 oz. tortellini). Add tortellini stirring with a wooden spoon and cook until they are "al dente."

3. Remove from heat, blend in 1 teaspoon butter and 2 tablespoons freshly grated Parmigiano (optional).

VARIATIONS:
   a) Use sour cream.
   b) With the cream, mix enough tomato sauce to make the mixture a pink color.

MACCHERONI ALLA BESCIAMELLA

Maccheroni with Besciamella

12 oz. maccheroni, thin but long	**4 tablespoons freshly grated**
2 rounded tablespoons butter	**Parmigiano, or**
1 rounded tablespoon flour	**grated Gruviera**
Milk as needed	**Sea salt**

1. Cook maccheroni in boiling water until "al dente."

2. Before pasta is done, prepare a medium thick Besciamella (see page 1). Remove from heat; blend in cheese and remaining butter.

3. Drain maccheroni; blend in sauce.

Taste for seasoning; serve at once.

FETTUCCINE AL BURRO
Egg Noodles with Butter and Cheese

8 tablespoons butter, softened
1/4 cup heavy cream
1/2 cup freshly grated
   imported Parmigiano
6 to 8 qts. water

1 tablespoon Sea salt
1 pound fettuccine
1 can white truffles (see
   "Herbs" page xxi), sliced
   very thin or finely chopped

1. Cream the butter by beating vigorously against sides of a heavy bowl with a wooden spoon until it is light and fluffy.

2. Beat in cream a little at a time; then a few tablespoons at a time. Then beat in 1/2 cup cheese.

3. Cover bowl and set aide. (If you don't use sauce at once, place in refrigerator; bring sauce to room temperature before tossing it with pasta.)

4. Place a large serving bowl or casserole in a 250 degree oven to warm while you cook fettuccine. To cook pasta, bring water to a bubbling boil in a large pot. Drop in fettuccine and stir gently with a wooden fork for a few minutes to prevent the strands from sticking to one another or to bottom of pot. Cook over high heat, stirring occasionally, until pasta is "al dente" (just tender).

5. Immediately drain pasta by lifting strands with 2 forks. Transfer at once to the warmed serving bowl.

6. Add butter-and-cream sauce and toss with fettuccine until it is well coated.

Season with pepper and truffles. Serve immediately.

PASTA E FAGIOLINI VERDI

Pasta with Green Beans

12 oz. spaghetti or linguine
2 small new potatoes, cut
  into very thin slices

1 hand-full fresh green beans,
  very thin
Pesto Sauce (see page 73)
1 tablespoon cream

1. Bring salted water to a boil in a large pot; drop in pasta, potatoes and beans. Cook until tender. Drain all ingredients together.

2. In a serving bowl, mix Pesto sauce and cream; add pasta, beans and potatoes; mix well.

PASTA AI QUATTRO FORMAGGI

Pasta with Four Cheeses

12 oz. maccheroni, zite,
  or spaghetti
2 oz. butter
2 oz. freshly grated
  Parmigiano

6 oz. assorted cheeses in equal
  parts; for example: Parmigiano,
  Gruviera, Holland cheese (or
  Provolone) and Mozzarella,
  cut into very thin sticks

1. Cook pasta until "al dente."

2. Mix equal parts of four cheeses.

3. Season with melted butter, Parmigiano and four cheeses.

PASTA ALLA RICOTTA
Pasta with Ricotta

12 oz. penne or small
   maccheroni
5 oz. Ricotta
Pinch of nutmeg

Pinch of sugar (optional)
Sea salt
2 tablespoons cream

1. Cook the pasta until "al dente." Drain.

2. Mix together Ricotta, salt, sugar, nutmeg and cream. Taste for seasoning.

3. Toss pasta with Ricotta cream.

SPAGHETTI ALL'AGLIO
Spaghetti with Oil and Garlic

12 oz. spaghetti
4 tablespoons pure olive oil
4 cloves garlic, cut into pieces
2 tablespoons freshly
   minced parsley

1 oz. freshly grated
   Parmigiano
1 oz. butter
Black pepper

1. In a large pot, cook spaghetti in abundant boiling water until "al dente." Drain.

2. In a small saucepan, heat oil over very low heat; sauté garlic (do not brown!); remove garlic. Cool oil 1 or 2 minutes. Add parsley.

3. Toss spaghetti with oil and parsley. Mix in Parmigiano, uncooked butter and pepper. Serve immediately.

SPAGHETTI ALLA CAVALLEGGERA

Spaghetti with Eggs and Cream

12 oz. spaghetti
3 egg yolks
3 tablespoons freshly
   grated Parmigiano

2 tablespoons cream
1 oz. butter
Pinch of nutmeg

1. Cook spaghetti in plenty of water until "al dente." Drain.

2. In a cup, mix egg yolks, Parmigiano, cream and nutmeg.

3. Toss spaghetti with this sauce and uncooked butter. Serve immediately.

SPAGHETTI AL PECORINO

Spaghetti with Pecorino Cheese

12 oz. spaghetti
3 1/2 oz. Pecorino Romano,
   freshly grated

Sea salt
Black pepper

1. Cook spaghetti in plenty of water until "al dente."

2. In a serving bowl, mix cheese with 3 tablespoons of cooking water.

3. Drain spaghetti and place in serving bowl; mix well with cheese and pepper. Serve immediately.

SPAGHETTI ALLE NOCI

Spaghetti with Walnut Sauce

12 oz. spaghetti
6 tablespoons pure olive oil
8 shelled walnuts, minced
2 tablespoons pine nuts,
  minced

2 cloves garlic, cut into
  2 or 3 pieces
2 tablespoons thick cream

1. Cook spaghetti in plenty of water until "al dente."

2. Heat oil and sauté garlic over low heat (do not brown!); then remove it.

3. Sauté walnuts and pine nuts in oil; cook 2 or 3 minutes over high heat, stirring constantly.

4. Drain spaghetti; mix nuts with cream; toss with spaghetti; mix well. Serve immediately.

PASTA WITH CURRY

12 oz. spaghetti or tagliatelle
2 tablespoons butter, or
  4 tablespoons pure olive oil
1 tablespoon flour
1 cup milk

1 teaspoon curry
1/2 cup cream
2 tablespoons freshly
  grated Parmigiano
Sea salt (optional)

1. Cook pasta in plenty of water until "al dente."

2. In a small saucepan, mix 1 tablespoon butter, flour and enough milk to make a thick Besciamella sauce (see page 1).

3. Add cream and curry; continue cooking, stirring, until sauce is done. Remove from heat; add remaining butter (uncooked) and Parmigiano.

4. Drain the pasta and toss with sauce.

TAGLIATELLE ALLA SALSA DI FORMAGGIO

Tagliatelle with Cheese Sauce

12 oz. tagliatelle	2 tablespoons cream
3 oz. Parmigiano	1/8 teaspoon Nutmeg
1 1/2 oz. butter	Sea salt (optional)
3 tablespoons milk	

1. Cook tagliatelle in plenty of water, salted, until "al dente."

2. In a small saucepan, combine 2 oz. freshly grated Parmigiano and 1 oz. Parmigiano cut into very small pieces; add nutmeg, milk and cream. Cook over very low heat. Make a thick sauce. Keep it warm over very low heat, stirring constantly.

3. Drain tagliatelle; toss with sauce and pieces of butter.

AREZZO (Tuscany): *Countryside at the foot of the Appennini mountains. The area has forests of chestnut, beech and fir trees. Olive oil and grapes are cultivated in the hills. Tarred, quiet country roads pass through small farming villages with their three-storied houses and painted wooden shutters resembling the windows of Swiss chalets.*

Vegetable Dishes

The recipes in this chapter are easy to prepare and, more importantly, very nutritious. Below are several useful suggestions to consider when preparing vegetables and legumes. Unless otherwise specified, recipes in this book serve four people.

1. Cook all fresh vegetables in salted boiling water. Exceptions are potatoes and dry legumes which should be started in cold water.

2. Cook green vegetables covered, in plenty of water over high heat. Generally, vegetables are done when tender, "al dente." Do not overcook!

3. Potatoes must be cooked over medium-low heat. You can only prepare them a few hours in advance. Uncooked, peeled potatoes tend to brown when exposed to the air for several hours; if cooked, they tend to become rancid.

4. Leftover cooked vegetables are excellent as cold salads; you can season them with Vinaigrette sauce (pure olive oil, vinegar, salt, pepper), or Citronnette sauce (pure olive oil, lemon, salt, pepper). These combinations can be served as antipastos.

5. Leftover, cooked vegetables can also be served as a side dish; place them in a casserole, sprinkle them with freshly grated Parmigiano, add melted butter; place casserole in very hot oven for 10 minutes, or until the vegetables are au gratin.

6. To eliminate the odor when boiling cabbage and cauliflower, you can place a cloth soaked in vinegar under the cover.

BATTER FOR FRIED VEGETABLES

This recipe is enough for 4 portions of vegetables. Combine and beat well:

4 oz. flour	**Sea salt**
2 tablespoons pure olive oil	**Water, enough to make**
1 egg, whole	**a soft mixture**

Coat the following vegetables in batter and deep fry.
- a) Tender celery sticks that have been cooked in salted boiling water for only 5-8 minutes;
- b) Thin strips of carrots, cooked, a fork full at a time;
- c) Slices of tomato, about 1 inch thick. When fried, season with salt, pepper, freshly minced parley;
- d) Thin slices or sticks of zucchini, marinated in advance for 2 hours in oil, lemon, salt;
- e) Thin slices of eggplant, peeled and salted;
- f) Slices of tender artichoke, 1/4 inch thick.

ASPARAGUS (1)

Serve cooked, warm and drained asparagus with:
- a) Pure olive oil only.
- b) Oil, salt, pepper.
- c) Oil, lemon, freshly minced parley, salt, pepper.
- d) Sprinkle the tips of asparagus with plenty of freshly grated Parmigiano; pour over them warm, slightly braised butter. Accompany this dish with fried eggs.
- e) Make several layers of asparagus, sprinkle each layer with freshly grated Parmigiano and warm, light-brown butter. Place in a 400 degree oven for 2-3 minutes, or until they are au gratin. Accompany this dish with fried eggs.
- f) Cover asparagus tips with zabaglione (see page 145) prepared with white wine instead of Marsala, no sugar, a pinch of salt, and flakes of butter.
- g) With Maltese sauce (see page 8).

ASPARAGUS (2)

Well drained, cold asparagus can be served with one of the following sauces: Mousseline, Maltese, Chantilly, Cream and Mustard, Vinegrette, Citronnette (see pages 7, 8, 9, 11, 12).

ARTICHOKES (BOILED)

While many people cook the artichokes in salted water, I suggest a simple addition which gives the artichokes a different, but very good flavor: Add to salted water, 1 or 2 tablespoons of flour, 3 or 4 drops of lemon juice and 1 tablespoon pure olive oil.

1. Clean and cut artichokes into quarters; soak them in cold water and the juice of 1/2 lemon. Drain.

2. Place in cold water over high heat and bring to a boil. Cook 25-30 minutes or until done.

3. Drain and gently squeeze by hand to eliminate all water.

FLAVORING METHODS:
   a) Warm or cold, serve with a sauce made of pure olive oil, lemon juice, pepper, salt and freshly minced parley.
   b) Warm or cold, serve with a Vinaigrette sauce (see page 11); if you wish, add freshly minced parsley.
   c) Sauté in butter; season with freshly grated Parmigiano.
   d) Lay them in a greased casserole, pour over melted butter, sprinkle with freshly grated Parmigiano; place in moderate oven until the cheese is au gratin.
   e) Serve warm with Salsa Maitre-d'hotel (see page 2).
   f) Lay artichokes in a greased casserole; cover with salsa Morney (see page 2); sprinkle with freshly grated Parmigiano or Gruviera, garnish with flakes of butter; place in hot oven until golden brown.
   g) Cold - with Cream and Mustard sauce (see page 7).

CARCIOFI ALLA PANNA
Artichokes with Cream

1. Cook 8 artichokes as suggested in "Artichokes (Boiled)," page 85, until just tender ("al dente"); drain well; place in a saucepan with a small amount of butter, cook over low heat until done.

2. Transfer artichokes to a serving dish; in the saucepan add cream (1 1/2 tablespoon for each artichoke); salt slightly; simmer to reduce liquid by 1/3. Pour over artichokes. Serve at once.

CARCIOFI AL VINO BIANCO
Artichokes with White Wine

This recipe has a very special taste.

1. Prepare and soak 8 artichokes as indicated in "Artichokes (Boiled)," page 85. Tightly pack artichokes in a saucepan; cover 3/4 of their depth with half water and half dry white wine. Add 2 cloves of garlic (optional), 2 tablespoons pure olive oil, salt.

2. Cover and cook over medium heat 30 minutes; occasionally check the quantity of liquid, add warm water if needed. At the end of cooking time, taste for seasoning.

3. Artichokes should not be bitter; if they are, correct the flavor with a pinch of sugar. Remove garlic. Do not overcook!

CARCIOFI STUFATI

Stewed Artichokes

1. Prepare 8 artichokes as described in "Artichokes (Boiled)," page 85. Sauté in pure olive oil over moderate heat. Cover and continue cooking over very low heat; occasionally, add warm water and 2 tablespoons of dry, white wine to artichokes.

2. When almost done, you may season them, with fresh minced Italian basil, marjoram or fresh parsley. If you wish, you may opt for a hot powdered pepper.

CARCIOFI IN FRICASSEA

Fricassed Artichokes

8 artichokes
2 oz. butter, or 3 tablespoons
   pure olive oil
3 egg yolks
2 tablespoons cream
1 tablespoon freshly
   grated Parmigiano

1 teaspoon lemon juice
1 tablespoon freshly
   minced parsley
Sea salt

1. Prepare artichokes as described in "Artichokes (Boiled)," page 85. Over moderate heat, melt butter in a deep saucepan; add well drained artichokes; salt and cook, stirring frequently; add 1 tablespoon of warm water at a time for 20 minutes, or until tender.

2. In a small bowl, beat egg yolks, cream, cheese, lemon juice. parsley and a pinch of salt. Two minutes before serving, lower heat and add this mixture to the artichokes; let thicken over very low heat, stirring continually.

Taste for seasoning; serve at once.

CAROTE CRUDE ALL'OLIO E LIMONE

Raw Carrots with Oil and Lemon

Cut carrots into slices. Season with pure olive oil, salt, lemon juice and pepper.

CAROTE AL BURRO

Carrots with Butter

1 1/2 lb. carrots	**Sugar**
2 oz. butter	**Sea salt**
1/2 tablespoon flour	

1. Prepare and wash carrots. Cut them into thick slices.

2. Melt butter in a saucepan; add carrots and stir; season with salt and a pinch of sugar; blend in flour; add water to barely cover carrots.

3. Bring to a boil, then lower to moderate heat and cook, covered, 20-30 minutes, or until tender.

4. Remove from heat; garnish with flakes of butter and a pinch of freshly minced parsley.

CAROTE ALLA CANNELLA

Carrots with Cinnamon

1. Prepare as in the "Carrots with Butter," above. Add salt, sugar, and a pinch of cinnamon.

2. When done, season carrots with lemon juice; eliminate parsley.

Taste for seasoning. Serve at once.

CAROTE ALLA PANNA
Carrots with Cream

Prepare as in the recipe "Carrots with Butter" (see page 88).

1. In a saucepan, melt butter (or use pure olive oil); add slices of carrots; season with salt and a pinch of sugar. Add water to barely cover the carrots. Cook covered over moderate heat, stirring occasionally.

2. When almost done, drain, then add 7 ounces of cream; finish cooking over high heat.

Taste for seasoning. Serve at once.

PUREA DI PATATE E CAROTE
Purée of Potatoes and Carrots

About 1 1/2 lb. total, serves 4

1. Peel and cut 3/4 lb. of boiling potatoes into thick slices; prepare and wash 3/4 lb. of carrots in salted water; cut into pieces. Cook potatoes and carrots separately. Drain well.

2. Purée potatoes and carrots, blend together well.

3. In a casserole, heat 2 oz. of butter; add 1 cup of cream; simmer, do not boil.

4. Add purée to casserole. Blend well.

Taste for seasoning. Serve at once.

CAULIFLOWER

1. Buy a compact, white flower. A cauliflower is fresh when green leaves are attached to it. A whole cauliflower weighing about 2 1/2 pounds cooks in 30 minutes. Cut off the stem; remove leaves; cut a deep cross in the bottom of the cauliflower.

2. Place cauliflower straight up in a pot; add enough water to cover half the cauliflower. To reduce the odor, place a cloth soaked in vinegar, under the cover. Cook until almost done.

Here are several quick flavoring methods. You may use pure olive oil instead of butter. Serve warm:

a) Pour about 2 oz. of melted butter over cauliflower.

b) Pour melted butter and minced fine herbs over cauliflower . (See Fine Herbs, pages xix, xx, xxi.)

c) Mix about 3/4 cup of warm, slightly salted cream, seasoned with a pinch of nutmeg and pepper. Pour over cauliflower.

d) Cut cauliflower into small pieces, sauté in 4 tablespoons of butter; sprinkle with freshly minced parsley.

e) Sauté small pieces of cauliflower in butter; sprinkle with freshly grated Parmigiano.

CAVOLFIORE AL GRATINO

Cauliflower au Gratin

1. Lay small pieces of cooked cauliflower in a greased casserole.

2. Cover with Salsa Morney (see page 2). Sprinkle with freshly grated Gruviera cheese, freshly grated bread and small flakes of butter.

3. Place in moderate oven until golden brown. Serve at once.

CAVOLFIORE CON SALSE
Cauliflower with Sauces

Cooked cauliflower, whole or cut into pieces, can be served with the following sauces:

- a) Salsa Maitre-d'hotel, page 2.
- b) Salsa Mousseline, page 7.
- c) Warm or cold, cauliflower is excellent with Vinaigrette sauce (mix pure olive oil, vinegar, pepper and a pinch of powdered mustard).

PUREA DI CAVOLFIORE
Purée of Cauliflower

1. Cook cauliflower until just tender. After having removed the short stems, process the flowerettes in a blender.

2. Transfer mixture to a saucepan with a small amount of butter; cook 2-3 minutes over medium heat, stirring, until liquid is absorbed.

3. Season with 1 cup of cream, salt, nutmeg, pepper.

Taste for seasoning. Serve at once.

CAVOLO ROSSO BRASATO

Braised Red Cabbage

1 red cabbage
   (about 2 1/2 pounds)
4 tablespoons pure olive oil
1-2 tablespoons vinegar
1 tablespoon sugar
Zest of 1 orange

3 large green apples, unpeeled,
   cut into thick slices
   (remove core)
Sea salt
Pepper
Nutmeg
Cinnamon

1. Remove old leaves and core of cabbage; cut into small strips, not too thin; wash and drain well.

2. Heat oil in a deep saucepan; add cabbage and cook 5 minutes over medium heat. Add remaining ingredients.

3. Cook, uncovered for 5 minutes, stirring well. Cover and cook over low heat for 40 minutes; if necessary, add 1-2 tablespoons of warm water.

Taste for seasoning.

CAVOLO AL CURRY

Cabbage with Curry

Serves 6

1 large Savoy or white cabbage	1 cup white dry wine
4 tablespoons pure olive oil	1 tablespoon sugar
1 medium onion, sliced	3 teaspoons curry
1 cup vinegar	Sea salt

1. Remove old leaves and core; wash well; drain; cut into small strips, not too thin.

2. Warm oil in large saucepan; add onion and cook until soft and transparent.

3. Add cabbage. Cook over medium heat until cabbage has absorbed oil.

4. Add vinegar, wine, sugar and curry. Cook, covered, over very low heat, for 1 1/2 hours, stirring occasionally. When almost done, reduce liquid over high heat (if necessary).

Taste for seasoning.

CUCUMBERS

Buy fresh, firm cucumbers. Peel and cut into slices. Flavor uncooked cucumbers with:
   a) pure olive oil;
   b) pure olive oil, lemon juice, salt;
   c) pure olive oil, vinegar, salt;
   d) cream, salt;
   e) cream, lemon juice, salt.

Cooked cucumbers: Cut into cubes; sauté in butter (2 oz. for about 1 pound), or 3 tablespoons of pure olive. Cook over medium heat for 30 minutes. When almost done, pour in 1/2 cup cream.

CIPOLLE AL LATTE E PANNA

Onions with Milk and Cream

Serves 1

1 medium onion
1 teaspoon butter, or
    1 tablespoon pure olive oil

Milk (as necessary)
1 1/2 tablespoons cream
Sea salt

1. Peel onions; cut into slices.

2. Melt butter in saucepan; add onions and brown lightly over medium-low heat; salt sparingly.

3. Add milk to barely cover onions; bring to a boil. Lower heat and cook over very low heat for about 20 minutes.

4. Before serving, reduce liquid over high heat, if necessary. Add cream; warm.

Taste for seasoning.

CIPOLLINE ALLA PANNA

Small Onions with Cream

1 lb. small onions, peeled
2 oz. butter or 3 tablespoons
    pure olive oil
Pinch of vegetable bouillon cube
1/2 tablespoon flour

1 cup cream
1/3 of the zest of a lemon,
    grated
Pinch of nutmeg
Sea salt

1. Melt butter in a saucepan until it foams; make a layer of onions not too packed; brown lightly on both sides.

2. Remove from heat and cool slightly. Sprinkle with flour, blend well.

3. Place over moderate heat; add a little water and bouillon, stirring until dissolved. Bring to a boil; lower heat, cover and cook for 30 minutes, or until onions are soft.

4. Add cream and salt; season with grated lemon zest, sprinkle with grated nutmeg. Reduce to moderate heat and cook for 15 minutes. When onions are done, the sauce must be plentiful.

Taste for seasoning.

CIPOLLINE STUFATE

Stewed Small Onions

1 lb. small onions, peeled	Pinch of vegetable bouillon cube
2 oz. butter, or 3 tablespoons pure olive oil	1 tablespoon flour
	Sea salt

1, 2, 3. As in "Small Onions with Cream," page 84, but cook 3/4 hour longer, or until onions are very soft. Salt. Taste for seasoning.

DRY WHITE BEANS

Follow the package instructions for cooking method. Drain and serve with:
a) pure olive oil, salt, pepper;
b) melted butter;
c) melted butter and cream.

TOSCANELLI AL POMODORO

Toscanelli (Italian) White Beans with Tomato

12 ounces beans serves 6

1. Cook beans; drain well.

2. In a saucepan, heat 5 tablespoons of pure olive oil; add 2-3 cloves of garlic and a sprig of fresh rosemary. Cook over low heat until garlic is slightly brown. Remove garlic. Add beans.

3. Thin 3 teaspoons of Italian tomato paste (Pomi brand) with a little warm water and add to beans.

4. Reduce liquid over moderate heat. Remove rosemary.

Taste for seasoning.

GREEN BEANS

Cook in salted boiling water until tender. Drained well and warm, season as follows:

    a) Sauté in warm butter or pure olive oil (4 oz. butter, or 5 tablespoons of pure olive oil, for about 1 pound beans).

    b) Sauté in butter or pure olive oil. Just before serving, sprinkle with minced garlic and fresh parsley; or minced parsley and basil.

    c) Sauté in butter or pure olive oil; then raise heat and cook until slightly brown; sprinkle with freshly grated Parmigiano (2 oz. for 1 pound beans); continue cooking over medium-high heat 1-2 minutes, stirring until beans are coated with cheese.

    d) Season with this sauce: Beat together 2 egg yolks, 2 tablespoons water, juice of 1 lemon, salt, pepper; cook in small saucepan over very low heat until the sauce is thick (do not boil!). Pour immediately over beans; serve at once.

    e) Drain, add cream (enough to barely cover the beans), and heat.

Cold, serve with:

    a) Salsa Vinaigrette (pure olive oil, vinegar, salt, pepper).

    b) Salsa Citronnette (pure olive oil, lemon juice, salt, pepper).

    c) Rouille Sauce or Citronnette (see pages 8 or 12).

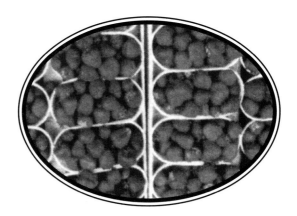

FENNELS

Buy young, tender fennels; remove hard leaves; cut off the stem and extremities; cut into quarters; cook in a generous amount of salted water over high heat for 15-20 minutes, or until well done. Drain.

SEASONING METHODS:

a) Sauté in pure olive oil and garlic until golden brown.

b) Place in serving dish and sauté in butter or pure olive oil until golden brown (about 2 oz. butter or 4 tablespoons of pure olive oil for 4 fennels); sprinkle with freshly grated Parmigiano; place in 350 degrees oven until cheese has formed a thin crust.

c) Sauté in butter or pure olive oil; sprinkle with freshly grated Parmigiano; add a small amount of cream. Place in a casserole and bake in 350 degree oven until cream-and-cheese sauce is thick.

d) Season with slightly braised butter or pure olive oil (2 oz. of butter or 4 tablespoons of pure olive oil for 3 fennels); complete with a pinch of salt, pepper, lemon juice and freshly minced parsley.

VARIATIONS:

e) Cook 10 minutes; drain. Cover and continue cooking over low heat in a generous amount of butter or pure olive oil; season with salt, pepper. When cooked, sprinkle with fresh minced parsley, Italian basil or oregano.

f) Wash and quarter fennels. Place in a saucepan. Add a mixture of half water and half white wine, salt and oregano, leaving the top quarter of the fennel exposed. Cover and cook over medium heat, 20-30 minutes, or until tender. (This dish has a very special taste.)

g) Cook 10 minutes; drain. In a saucepan, heat 2-3 tablespoons olive oil; add the fennels and cook 5 minutes over moderate heat; add 1 teaspoon of oregano. Continue cooking until fennels are tender.

h) Cook 10 minutes; drain. Place fennel in melted butter or pure olive oil (3 oz. of butter or 4 tablespoons of pure olive oil for 4 fennels) and cook additional 10 minutes. Transfer into serving dish; add 1 cup of heated and slightly salted cream.

FUNGHI "PORCINI" ALLA PAESANA
Porcini Mushrooms with Garlic

1. Cut 2 pounds of mushrooms into slices not too thin.

2. In a saucepan, sauté 2 garlic cloves in 8 tablespoons of pure olive; remove garlic when slightly brown.

3. Add mushrooms; sauté 5-7 minutes on medium-high heat.

4. Add salt and pepper; cook over moderate heat 10 minutes, or until mushrooms are done.

5. Before serving, sprinkle with freshly minced parsley and drops of lemon juice.

Taste for seasoning. Serve at once.

FRIED MUSHROOMS

For this recipe, you use only mushroom caps. Wash and cut them into slices 1/4 inch wide. Coat in flour; fry in hot, pure olive oil until golden brown. Remove and drain oil from mushrooms; sprinkle with salt.

Taste for seasoning. Serve immediately.

FUNGHI "OVOLI" ALLA RABBÌ
Oven-Baked Mushrooms and Potatoes

1. Wash mushrooms. Grease a large pan well with pure olive oil. Make a layer of thinly sliced new potatoes; salt lightly.

2. Over the layer of potatoes, place mushrooms caps, tightly packed; add half the stems, sliced.

3. Mince remaining stems and mix with fresh minced parsley and a pinch of garlic. Sprinkle this mixture over mushrooms; add a pinch of oregano, salt, and plenty of pure olive oil.

4. Add 1/2 cup of water and 1/2 cup of dry white wine.

5. Transfer to oven; bake at 350 degrees 30-40 minutes, or until done.

FUNGHI STUFATI
Stewed Mushrooms

1 lb. Shiitake, dry Mushrooms (Champignon Séchè)
2 oz. butter, or 3 tablespoons pure olive oil

1. Follow the package instructions for cooking mushrooms.

2. In a skillet, heat butter or oil; add mushrooms; sauté 3-4 minutes over medium-high heat.

3. Lower heat; salt, cover. Cook 7-10 minutes, or until mushrooms are tender.

VARIATIONS:
   a) 1,2, as above. Lower heat; sprinkle with 1 tablespoon of flour, stirring to blend; add 8 oz. of cream. Cover and cook 7-10 minutes. Remove from heat; add 1/4 cup of cream and 1 teaspoon butter or 3 tablespoons pure olive oil. Blend well.
   b) 1,2, as above. Lower heat; add 1-2 tablespoons of lemon juice. Cover and cook 7-10 minutes until mushrooms are tender.
   c) 1,2, as above. Lower heat; add 1-2 tablespoons of lemon juice and a pinch of minced thyme. Cover and cook 7-10 minutes or until mushrooms are tender.

FUNGHI IN FRICASSEA
Fricasseed Mushrooms

**1 lb. Shiitake, dried mushrooms
(Champignon Séchè)**
1 egg yolk
**2 oz. butter + 1 teaspoon
of butter**

5 tablespoons cream
1 tablespoon lemon juice
Sea salt
Pepper

1. Prepare mushrooms for cooking, following package instructions.

2. In a skillet, heat 2 oz. butter; add mushrooms; sauté 3-4 minutes over medium-high heat.

3. Lower heat. Cover and cook 7-10 minutes or until mushrooms are just tender.

4. In a small bowl, beat together egg yolks, cream, pinch of salt; lemon juice, pepper.

5. Pour mixture over mushrooms and cook over low heat (do not boil!) until sauce is condensed.

6. Remove from heat; add 1 teaspoon of butter, stirring vigorously. Taste for seasoning. Serve at once.

FUNGHI FREDDI AL COGNAC

Cold Mushrooms with Cognac

This is an excellent recipe!

14 oz. Shiitake, dried mushrooms (Champignon Séchè)
4 tablespoons pure olive oil
1 bay leaf
1 clove of carnation
1 sprig rosemary

1 clove garlic
2 tablespoons Cognac
Sea salt
Pepper
Juice of 1/2 lemon

1. Prepare mushrooms for cooking, following package instructions.

2. Sauté 2 minutes in hot oil.

3. In a small pot, warm Cognac, then light it; pour over mushrooms.

4. Combine other ingredients and add to mushrooms. Lower heat, cover; cook 10 minutes. Remove garlic and bay leaf. Taste for seasoning.

5. Cool mushrooms. Serve as antipasto or side dish.

CREMA DI INDIVIA

Endive with Cream

1 1/2 lb. endive (remove stem and outer leaves; wash)
2 oz. butter, or 4 tablespoons pure olive oil

1/4 cup cream
Sea salt

1. Add endive to a pot of salted, boiling water. Cook 30 minutes.

2. Drain well; squeeze out residual water by hand.

3. Melt butter in a skillet; add endive; sauté to light golden brown on both sides, (10 - 15 minutes).

4. Place into serving dish; cover with slightly salted warm cream.

Taste for seasoning.

INDIVIA AL LIMONE
Endive with Lemon

1 1/2 lb. endive (remove stem
    and outer leaves; wash)
4 oz. butter, or 5 tablespoons
    pure olive oil

Juice of 1/2 lemon
Sea salt

1, 2, as in preceding recipe.

3. As in preceding recipe, using 2 oz. butter.

4. Place endive in a serving dish. In a small pan, heat 2 oz. butter until light brown; add lemon juice. Pour over endive.

INDIVIA AL FORNO
Baked Endive

1 1/2 lb. endive (remove stem
    and outer leaves; wash)
3 oz. butter, or 5 tablespoons
    pure olive oil
Sea salt
3 tablespoons freshly
    grated Parmigiano
1 pinch vegetable bouillon
    dissolved in water

3 tablespoons cream
1 large cup of Besciamella
    made with:
- 2 tablespoons butter, or
    4 tablespoons pure olive oil
- 2 tablespoons (scant) flour
- 1 1/2 cup milk

1, 2, as in preceding recipes.

3. As in preceding recipes, using 2 oz. butter.

4. Prepare a medium Besciamella (see ingredients above) adding vegetable bouillon and cream.

5. Cover endive with Besciamella; sprinkle with freshly grated Parmigiano and remaining butter cut into small pieces.

6. Place in 350 degrees oven for 10 minutes, or until the top is slightly brown.

LENTICCHIE ALLA BORGHESE

Lentils and Onions

1/2 lb. lentils, cooked until tender, drained	1 onion, minced
6 tablespoons pure olive oil	Pepper
	Sea salt

1. Combine all ingredients in a saucepan; add 1 cup warm water.

2. Cook until tender. If necessary, add a small amount of warm water, stirring well by lifting lentils from bottom of pot. Taste for seasoning.

LENTICCHIE AL POMODORO

Lentils with Tomatoes

Same ingredients as in preceding recipe; plus 2-3 tablespoons of Italian tomato paste (Pomi brand) and 2 cloves of garlic.

1. Heat oil; over moderate heat, sauté garlic cloves and onion, (do not brown).

2. Remove garlic. Add lentils; sauté over moderate heat, stirring carefully with a wooden spoon.

3. Add tomato paste thinned in 1 cup of warm water. Continue cooking over very low heat, stirring carefully, when needed. If necessary, add a little warm water.

Taste for seasoning.

MELANZANE AL FORNO
Baked Eggplant

This dish is excellent!

1. Remove stems of 2 medium eggplants; wash. Cut in half lengthwise. With the tip of a small knife, make deep, crisscross cuts around edges.

2. Marinate eggplants with pure olive oil, minced garlic and minced oregano. Let stand for 1 hour.

3. Lay eggplants cut side up in well oiled saucepan; pour more oil over eggplants. Cook in moderate oven for 30 minutes, or until done. Salt.

MELE AL BURRO

Apples with Butter

1. Peel 5 yellow apples; remove core; cut into 1/4 inch slices.

2. Coat lightly with flour. Over low heat, sauté apples in a generous amount of heated butter until slightly golden brown.

Taste for seasoning.

MELE ALLA CANNELLA
Apples with Cinnamon

1. Peel 5 apples (yellow or green); remove core; cut into quarters.

2. Place in saucepan and add water to half their depth; cook until barely soft.

3. Drain well. Return to heat; crush them with a fork over high heat, stirring, until liquid is evaporated.

4. Remove from heat; season with a little butter and a pinch of salt, sugar and cinnamon. Taste for seasoning.

BOILED POTATOES

Wash new potatoes; cover with cold water; let stand for 2 hours. Wash and drain. Place potatoes in a pot; salt; bring to a boil over high heat. Cook over low heat until just done.

Serve warm, sliced, with:
  a) Melted butter, only.
  b) Pure olive oil, only.
  c) Vinaigrette sauce (pure olive oil, vinegar, salt, pepper).
  d) Pure olive oil; thin slices of garlic (remove before serving), freshly minced parsley; cool; taste for seasoning; serve.
  e) Cover with freshly grated Parmigiano and very hot golden brown butter, or pure olive oil.

Cold, season with Mayonnaise thinned with cream or milk; blend in minced young onion.

PATATE NOCCIOLA
Small Potato Balls

1. Peel 2 pounds russet potatoes; wash in cold, salted water. Shape into small balls with a scooping spoon. Let stand in water for 2 hours before cooking. Rinse well.

2. In a saucepan, heat 8 tablespoons pure olive oil (do not brown); add potatoes and cook over high heat until golden brown. Lower heat, stirring slowly with a wooden spoon. Cook until done.

Taste for seasoning.

PATATE AL BASILICO

Potatoes with Basil

1 1/2 lb. new potatoes
5 oz. butter, or 1/2 cup
    pure olive oil

2 tablespoons fresh Italian
    basil, minced
Sea salt

1. Peel and wash potatoes; cut into quarters; cook in salted water until just tender; drain.

2. Transfer to a skillet with heated butter or oil; cook until done.

3. Remove from heat; sprinkle with basil.

Taste for seasoning.

PATATE ALL'OREGANO

Potatoes with Oregano

1,2, as in the preceding recipe.

3. When almost cooked, sprinkle with 1 teaspoon oregano. Taste for seasoning.

PATATE GRATINATE

Potatoes au Gratin

1 1/2 lb. new or russet potatoes
5 oz. butter, or 1/2 cup
   pure olive oil

3 oz. freshly grated Parmigiano
1 cup thick cream
Sea salt

1. Peel and wash potatoes. Cook in salted water until just tender; drain well.

2. In a saucepan heat butter or oil; add potatoes. Cook over medium heat as you crush potatoes with a fork.

3. Place a layer of potatoes in a casserole; sprinkle with cheese; cover cheese with cream.

4. Bake in 400 degree oven and cook until top is crusted.

PATATE AL LATTE

Potatoes with Milk

1 1/2 lb. new potatoes
4 oz butter, or 6 tablespoons
   pure olive oil

2 cups milk
Sea salt

1. Peel and wash potatoes; cut into small cubes.

2. In a saucepan, heat butter or oil; add potatoes. Brown slightly over high heat.

3. Add milk to barely cover potatoes, salt; bring to boil; lower heat to medium-low; cook 30 minutes. If necessary, add more milk.

Taste for seasoning.

PATATE TRIFOLATE DI MIA MADRE

Potatoes – My Mother's Recipe

1 1/2 lb. new potatoes
5 oz. butter
2 tablespoons pure olive oil

2 cloves garlic
2 tablespoons freshly
   minced parsley

1. Peel and wash potatoes; cut into 2 inch cubes.

2. Heat butter and oil in a frying pan with slightly crushed garlic.

3. Add potatoes, well dried with a cloth. Cook over moderate heat for 20-30 minutes, stirring frequently and carefully, until slightly golden brown; salt.

4. When potatoes are done, remove garlic. Remove from heat; add parsley, stir well.

Taste for seasoning.

TORTINO DI PATATE

Potato Cakes

1 pound new potatoes
3 oz. butter

2 tablespoons pure olive oil
Sea salt

1. Peel, wash and dry the potatoes; cut them into very thin slices; dry again.

2. In a large frying pan, heat butter and oil until hot. Add potatoes, making 1 uniform layer.

3. Cook over high heat until bottom of potatoes is golden brown; lower heat and cook 20 minutes without disturbing potatoes.

4. Place a dish over frying pan and turn the potatoes over. Slide potatoes back into pan and cook the other side 10-20 minutes, or until golden brown. Salt.

PATATE AL FORNO CON PAPRIKA

Baked Potatoes with Paprika

1 1/2 lb. new potatoes	Paprika
5 oz. butter, or 1/2 cup pure olive oil	Sea salt

1. Peel, wash and dry the potatoes; cut them into thin sticks.

2. Place in a casserole; cover with flakes of butter, pinch of salt, and 2 pinches of paprika.

3. Bake in hot oven and cook for 30-40 minutes, stirring frequently.

Taste for seasoning.

PATATE SABLÉES

Fricasseed of Potatoes

1 1/2 lb. new potatoes	1 tablespoon grated dry bread
5 oz. butter, or 1/2 cup pure olive oil	Sea salt
	Paprika

1. Peel, wash and dry the potatoes; cut them into 1 1/4 inch cubes; dry again.

2. Set aside 1 teaspoon butter. In a large skillet, heat remaining butter until very hot; add potatoes. Cook until slightly brown, stirring frequently, over moderate heat.

3. When almost done, season potatoes with a pinch of salt, a pinch of paprika and grated bread, blending well. Remove from heat; blend in reserved butter until melted.

Taste for seasoning.

LEEKS

Clean and cut 1 pound leeks into 1 1/2 inch lengths; cook in salted boiling water, until done.

Seasoning methods:
a) Place leeks in serving dish; cover with melted butter or pure olive oil (3 oz. butter or 5 tablespoons of pure olive oil for 1 pound leeks).
b) Place leeks in serving dish; add warm cream (7 oz. for 1 pound of leeks).
c) Place in serving dish; cover with soft Besciamella (see page 1).
d) Place in buttered dish; cover leeks with freshly grated Parmigiano and melted butter or pure olive oil; bake in 350 degree oven for 10 minutes.
e) Place in buttered dish; cover with Besciamella or Salsa Mornay (see pages 1 and 2); sprinkle with freshly grated Parmigiano (optional); and flakes of butter; place in hot oven for 10 minutes, or until a light crust is formed over Besciamella.
f) Cook leeks in warm butter or pure olive oil until golden brown; add cream to barely cover leeks; reduce heat and cook until cream is reduced to half.

Taste for seasoning.

PEPERONATA

Braised Peppers

14 oz. Italian canned stewed tomatoes

7 oz. sweet peppers, very firm (mix red, yellow and green for color)

2 cloves garlic, minced

4-5 tablespoons pure olive oil

Sea salt

1 teaspoon fresh Italian basil, minced

1. Wash peppers and remove seeds; dry very well; cut into strips.

2. Sauté garlic in oil over medium heat. Add peppers, cover and steam over medium-low heat for 20 minutes.

3. Add salt and pepper, tomatoes (with liquid), and basil; stir.

4. Cook uncovered, over moderate heat, until all liquid is absorbed.

Taste for seasoning. You can serve this dish either warm or cold.

PISELLI AL BURRO

Peas with Butter

1. Buy good quality frozen peas. Steam them in butter, over low heat, until just tender. Cook uncovered until liquid is evaporated.

2. Sprinkle with freshly minced parsley. Add a pinch of sugar to balance flavor. Taste for seasoning.

PISELLI ALLA PANNA

Peas with Cream

1. As in the preceding recipe.

2. Add 1/4 cup cream. Salt and cook over medium heat until cream is reduced to half.

Add a pinch of sugar to balance flavor. Taste for seasoning.

RATATOUILLE

Braised Vegetables

6 tablespoons pure olive oil

4 small onions, sliced

4 peppers, firm, pith and seeds removed, cut into large pieces

4 small zucchini, cut into 1/2 inch pieces

4 small eggplants, peeled and cut into 1/2 inch pieces

4 canned Italian tomatoes, chopped

Sea salt

Pepper

Fresh, minced parsley

Fresh, Italian minced basil

1. In a saucepan, heat oil; add onions; sauté over medium heat until soft and transparent, but not brown.

2. Add zucchini, eggplants, tomatoes, peppers. Cook, covered, over medium-low heat 15 minutes, or until vegetables are very soft. Stir frequently and gently to prevent scorching. Uncover, continue cooking until sauce thickens.

3. Season with salt and pepper. Taste for seasoning. Cool.

4. Before serving, sprinkle with freshly minced parsley and basil.

FRITTELLE DI SPINACI

Spinach Frittate

Serves 3

14 oz. pkg. frozen spinach
2 tablespoons Besciamella,
 firm (see page 1)
2 egg yolks
Sugar

Cinnamon
Zest of 1 lemon, grated
3 oz. butter and 5 tablespoons
 of pure olive oil
Freshly grated dry bread

1. Defrost spinach, squeeze to remove water; cut finely.

2. Combine Besciamella, egg yolks, sugar, cinnamon and lemon zest; add spinach; blend well. Taste for seasoning.

3. Form patties from spinach mixture and coat with bread crumbs.

4. In a fryer, heat oil and butter; add patties, cook over high heat until golden brown. Turn and cook the other side.

5. Drain from fat; place in a serving dish.

ZUCCHINE ALL'OLIO E LIMONE

Zucchini with Oil and Lemon

1. Buy small, firm zucchini. Wash them but do not peel, dry, cut into thin slices.

2. Marinate 1 hour in a generous amount of pure olive oil and lemon juice.

3. 15 minutes before serving, drain oil and lemon into a fryer; heat; add zucchini and cook over high heat until zucchini are just tender. Salt, pepper. Taste for seasoning.

ZUCCHINE ALLA PANNA E FORMAGGIO
Zucchini with Cream and Cheese

1. Buy small, firm zucchini. Wash them but do not peel; cut into 1 1/4 inch pieces. Place in salted, boiling water; cook until almost done. Drain.

2. Transfer to a saucepan; add plenty of butter or pure olive oil; cook to reduce liquid, stirring gently with a wooden spoon.

3. Add freshly grated Parmigiano blended in 1 cup of cream; stir zucchini over moderate heat until cheese is melted.

Taste for seasoning.

ZUCCHINE AL VINO BIANCO
Zucchini with White Wine

1. Buy small, firm zucchini; wash and cut into thin slices.

2. Place in saucepan; barely cover zucchini with half water and half white wine; add 1 tablespoon of oregano, 2 tablespoons pure olive oil and salt.

3. Bring to a boil and cook over medium heat until zucchini are tender. If necessary, continue cooking over high heat until liquid thickens. Taste for seasoning and serve.

ZUCCHINE IN FRICASSEA

Fricasseed Zucchini

1 1/2 lb. zucchini, washed,
   dried and thinly sliced
1 large onion, sliced
2 oz. butter, or 3 tablespoons
   pure olive oil

2 egg yolks
2 tablespoons cream
1 tablespoon lemon juice
Sea salt
Pepper

1. In a saucepan or casserole, melt butter over moderate heat; add onion; cook 2 minutes. Add zucchini.

2. Salt and cook, covered, over moderate heat, stirring frequently, for 30 minutes or until zucchini are tender. To prevent scorching, add a small amount of warm water.

3. A few minutes before serving, beat together egg yolk, lemon juice, a pinch of salt, pepper and cream. Lower heat; pour sauce over zucchini, stir gently. Continue cooking and stirring, over very low heat for 2-3 minutes, or until egg is cooked (do not boil!).

Taste for seasoning. Serve immediately.

TERRINA DI VERDURE, DI ANTONELLA

Baked Vegetables, Antonella's Recipe

Serves 5

Pure olive oil as needed
1/2 onion, minced
1/2 stalk celery, minced
2 carrots, minced
2 tablespoons fresh spinach, minced
1 clove garlic, minced
1/2 potato, minced
1/2 sprig of thyme

1/2 sprig of rosemary
1/2 cup white dry wine
1 tablespoon vegetable bouillon
1/2 pound Ricotta
1 tablespoon freshly grated Parmigiano
Nutmeg
1 tablespoon minced walnuts
2 eggs

1. In a saucepan, sauté onion, celery, carrots, spinach, garlic, potato, thyme and rosemary in pure olive oil, over medium low heat (do not brown). Stir in salt and pepper.

2. Add wine and bouillon; cook over medium heat until vegetables are tender, stirring frequently. Remove thyme and rosemary. Remove saucepan from heat; cool.

3. Mix together Ricotta, Parmigiano, a pinch of nutmeg, eggs and walnuts. Blend with vegetables. Place in buttered top double boiler. Bake in 375 degree oven for 1/2 hour, or until well done.

4. Set casserole aside to cool until mixture is lukewarm. Slice and serve with Cheese Sauce or Egg Sauce (see pages 6, 4).

INVOLTINI DI MELANZANE, DI ANTONELLA

Eggplant Rolls, Antonella's Recipe   *Serves 8*

4 large eggplants, peeled and
   cut into 1/2 inch slices
4 pounds Ricotta
1/4 pound freshly grated
   dry bread
1/4 pound freshly grated
   Parmigiano

3 eggs
Pinch fresh Italian basil, minced
Pinch fresh parsley, minced
Sea salt
Pepper

1. Salt eggplants; let stand 2 hours.

2. Wash eggplants and grill. Cool.

3. Mix well Ricotta, grated bread, Parmigiano, eggs, basil, parsley, salt, pepper. Cover cold slices of eggplants with mixture; roll each slice and secure with a toothpick. Place in a casserole.

4. Bake in a 375 degree oven for 1/2 hour. Serve with Tomato Sauce (1), page 71.

CELERY

Wash and cut celery. Bring plenty of water to a boil; add celery and cook over high heat 2-3 minutes only. Drain. Serving suggestions:
a) Finish cooking in butter or pure olive oil; place celery in a serving dish; drizzle with cooking fat.
b) In a casserole, heat butter or pure olive oil; add celery; sprinkle with freshly grated Parmigiano and freshly grated dry bread. Bread is optional or used sparingly. Bake in moderate oven until au gratin.
c) Cook in butter or pure olive oil until celery is golden brown; cover with liquid Besciamella sauce (see page 1).
d) Brown celery in butter or pure olive oil; cover with Besciamella sauce, (see page 1), freshly grated Parmigiano and a few drops of Worcesterhire sauce.

INSALATA DI POMODORO
Tomato Salad

Remember to season tomatoes just before serving. For a variety of taste:

a) Add uncooked onions to tomato rings.

b) Serve with a sauce made with pure olive oil, vinegar, salt, pepper, fresh parsley, fresh Italian basil, a small quantity of onion, a pinch of garlic. Process all ingredients in a blender. Pour over sliced tomatoes.

POMODORI SALTATI ALL'OLIO
Tomato Sautéed in Oil

1. Cut tomatoes in half crosswise; remove seeds and water.

2. In a frypan, heat a small amount of pure olive oil. Add tomatoes, cut side down; cook on high heat for 5 minutes. Turn and cook 7-10 minutes.

3. Mince and mix together fresh parsley, fresh Italian basil and a pinch of garlic.

4. Remove tomatoes to a serving dish with cut sides facing up; season with salt and pepper; sprinkle the herbs over tomatoes.

5. In the oil left in frying pan, sauté grated dry bread for 1 minute; sprinkle over tomatoes. Serve.

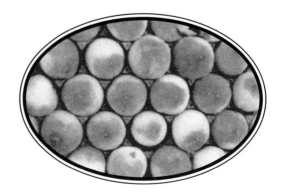

POMODORI E ANANASSO

Tomatoes Stuffed with Pineapple

8 small tomatoes

Slices of pineapple,
   cut into small pieces

6 walnuts, minced

Mayonnaise

Sea salt

Pepper

1. Cut tops of tomatoes; drain water and remove seeds; season with salt and pepper; let stand for 30 minutes.

2. Drain tomatoes again; fill them with small pieces of pineapple and walnuts mixed with Mayonnaise. Cover with more Mayonnaise; refrigerate for 2 hours before serving.

For more vegetable dishes, see also "Antipastos" chapter.

A *market shop in* CATANIA (Sicily).

Food and Wines. Sicily is well-known for its fine wines: Marsala, the classic dessert wine, Faro, Corvo bianco di Casteldaccia, and the red and white wines of Etna. Sicily's cuisine is strong and reflects the optimistic and rugged character of the Sicilians. Specialties are: Cannoli, cylindrical pastry cakes filled with ricotta cheese, cream, candied fruit or chocolate. Cassata, an ice-cream cake, with chocolate, custard and almonds. Frutta Candita, crystallized oranges, tangerines, figs and other fruit. Gelati, Sicilian ices are among the best in Italy, and often have fresh fruit as part of the ingredients.

Salads

Lettuce should not be cut with a knife: remove the core and leaves by hand. This rule does not apply when leaves must be cut into strips. To serve fresh and crisp lettuce, wash it, wrap it in plastic and refrigerate for at least 1/2 hour. Dress salad just before serving.

Unless otherwise specified, recipes in this book serve four people.

SAUCES FOR SALADS

See "Sauces" Chapter, pages 1 to 12.

INSALATA PRIMAVERA
Springtime Salad

1. Cook young carrots, potatoes, beets, hearts of artichokes, peas, tender asparagus, hearts of celery. Drain.

2. Dress vegetables with a good Mayonnaise; blend well. Place in serving dish; add more Mayonnaise. Garnish with olives, thin slices of lemon and small green lettuce leaves.

SALSA DI UOVA E FORMAGGIO
Dressing with Egg and Cheese

To serve with various types of lettuce.

1 egg yolk, uncooked
1 tablespoon freshly
   grated Parmigiano
1 teaspoon mustard,
   sweet or piquant

4 tablespoons pure olive oil
1 1/2 teaspoons lemon juice
1 teaspoon vinegar, sweet
Sea salt
White pepper

Mix well Parmigiano and egg yolk; blend in mustard. Add other ingredients, stirring lightly. Pour over lettuce; toss well.

INSALATA A MODO MIO
Salad My Way
Serves 3

2 heads of lettuce
2 oz. Gruviera cheese
6 tablespoons pure olive oil
1-2 tablespoons vinegar,
   or lemon juice

Pinch of fresh parsley, minced
Pinch of fresh Italian basil,
   minced
1 tablespoon onion, minced

1. Wash lettuce, drain and cut; wrap it in a cloth, refrigerate until ready to serve.

2. Mix basil, parsley and onion with oil, vinegar (or lemon), a pinch of salt and white pepper.

3. Cut Gruviera in small squares; add to parsley and onion; marinate 1 hour.

4. Before serving, place lettuce in a serving dish; cover with sauce; and toss well.

INSALATA AL GORGONZOLA

Gorgonzola Salad

2 small bunches chicory
1 1/2 oz. Gruviera cheese
1/2 oz. Gorgonzola, piquant
2-5 tablespoons pure olive oil
1-2 tablespoons vinegar

1 teaspoon mustard
1 teaspoon Cognac
Sea salt
Pepper

1. Wash chicory; drain; cut into thin strips; wrap in a cloth; refrigerate until ready to serve.

2. In a bowl, mix Gorgonzola and mustard with oil; stir in vinegar (or lemon juice), salt, pepper, Cognac.

3. Arrange chicory and Gruviera cheese in a salad bowl; add sauce; mix; serve immediately.

INSALATA DI ARANCE

Salad with Oranges

Peel and skin oranges; cut them into horizontal slices. Dress with their juice, Kirsch, salt and pepper; blend well.

INSALATA ESTIVA
Summer Salad

From the following list, select several ingredients, but always add tomatoes:

- **boiled potatoes (new or russet)**
- **green beans, boiled**
- **hard boiled eggs**
- **hearts of celery**
- **peppers**
- **rings of onion**
- **black or green olives (or both)**

Dress with Vinaigrette or Citronnette sauces (see pages 11, 12).

INSALATA DI SEDANI
Celery Salad

Cut tender stalks of celery into thin strips; 2 hours before serving, dress with Vinaigrette and Mustard sauce (see pages 11, 9).

INSALATA DI SPINACI
Spinach Salad

Use tender uncooked spinach and quartered tomatoes; dress with Cream of Citronnette sauce (see page 12). Garnish with hard boiled eggs.

INSALATA ALLA PANNA

Salad with Cream

Use hearts of lettuce, separate into quarters by hand; quartered hard boiled eggs; dress with Cream of Citronnette sauce (see page 12).

INSALATA ALLE MANDORLE

Salad with Almonds

Use 1 head of lettuce, 2 medium oranges, quartered (peeled and skinned), salted, slivered almonds:

1. Heat 4 oz. butter until slightly golden brown; stir in juice of 1 lemon.

2. Pour over lettuce and orange. Toss well.

INSALATA DI FUNGHI (1)

Raw Mushroom Salad (1)

1/2 pound fresh Porcini mushrooms, thinly sliced	1/4 cup thinly sliced scallion greens
2 teaspoons lemon juice	3 tablespoons pure olive oil
	Sea salt

In a serving bowl, toss the mushrooms with lemon juice until slices are lightly moistened. Add scallion greens, oil and salt; toss again. Chill before serving.

INSALATA DI FUNGHI (2)
Mushroom Salad, Ovoli or Porcini(2)

In a serving dish, season mushrooms with pure olive oil, salt and pepper. Garnish with lemon quarters. On the side, serve additional oil, if needed.

INSALATA DI FUNGHI (3)
Mushroom Salad (3)

1. Clean mushrooms; dry; cut into slices.

2. One hour before serving, season with pure olive oil, lemon juice, salt, pepper. Taste for seasoning.

3. Serve as antipasto or side dish.

INSALATA DI POMODORO
Tomato Salad

5 medium, firm ripe tomatoes, sliced 1/4 inch thick	1/4 teaspoon garlic, minced
1/2 cup pure olive oil	Sea salt
2 tablespoons wine vinegar, or lemon juice	Pepper
1 tablespoon fresh Italian basil, minced	2 tablespoons thinly sliced scallions
	1 tablespoon fresh Italian parsley, minced

Arrange tomatoes in overlapping circles on a platter. In a bowl, mix oil, vinegar, basil, garlic, salt, pepper. Blend well and pour mixture over tomatoes. Sprinkle with scallions and parsley.

For Salad Dishes see also "Antipastos" Chapter, page 15.

A Medieval street of a village in the MARCHE. This picture projects a perfect balance with the antique artistry of wrought iron and the Medieval arches built of colored brick. In the old shop one can buy colored ceramics and hand-painted wooden objects.

127

ORVIETO (Umbria). Built on a hill, this city is famous for her antiquity: the Etruscan necropolis, the Medieval streets and the magnificent architecture of the buildings, especially the Cathedral which comes very close to being as stunningly beautiful as the cathedral in Florence. Orvieto is also famous for colored ceramics; industries include wrought iron and embroidery.

Food and wines. *The region produces olive oil, wines and cereal. Well-known is the "Orvieto" wine - pale, golden-yellow and transparent with a delightfully sharp aftertaste.*

Cheese Dishes

The following dishes may be served as antipastos or side dishes.

*Unless otherwise specified,
recipes in this book serve four people.*

FONDUTA

Toast With Hot Melted Cheese   *Serves 4 to 6*

1 pound imported Fontina or
   Gruviera cheese, cut in
   small pieces
1 teaspoon cornstarch
   dissolved in 1/2 cup milk
Sea salt
1/8 teaspoon white pepper

3 egg yolks
1 can white truffles, thinly
   sliced (see "Herbs" page xxi)
4 to 6 slices white Italian or
   French bread, toasted,
   buttered and cut diagonally
   into triangles.

1. Put pieces of cheese, cornstarch and milk mixture, salt and pepper
   into a heavy 2-3 quart saucepan. Over low heat, cook and stir
   constantly, about 5 minutes, or until cheese melts.

2. Beat egg yolks slightly for a few seconds with a whisk or electric beater.
   Spoon 1/4 cup hot cheese mixture into yolks and beat vigorously.

3. Pour mixture slowly back into pan, beating constantly; continue
   cooking over low heat until mixture is smooth and thickens to a
   heavy consistency. Ladle immediately into heated soup bowls.

4. Arrange truffles on top of Fondue. Place toast around inside edges
   of bowls. Serve hot immediately.

MOZZARELLA IN CARROZZA
Deep-fried Cheese Sandwiches

Pure olive oil	**4 eggs**
1 pound loaf of Italian or	**1/4 cup milk**
French bread, sliced	**1 cup milk**
1 pound Mozzarella	**1 cup fine dry bread crumbs**

1. Heat 3-4 inches of oil in a deep frypan. Using a cookie cutter or small glass, cut slices of bread in 3 inch rounds. Slice Mozzarella 1/4 inch thick (slices must be smaller than circles of bread). Make sandwiches of bread and cheese.

2. In a small bowl, beat together eggs and 1/4 cup milk. Pour a cup of milk into another bowl; spread bread crumbs on wax paper. Dip each sandwich briefly in milk, press edges of bread together to seal them; coat both sides thoroughly with bread crumbs. Roll edges of sandwiches in bread crumbs to seal them.

3. Dip sandwiches, one at a time, in egg mixture; fry in hot oil until golden brown on each side. Drain on paper towel; serve hot.

RICOTTA ALLE ERBE
Ricotta with Herbs   *Serves 3*

1. Mix together well:

   - **3 1/2 oz. Ricotta**
   - **ample fresh Italian basil, minced**
   - **ample fresh parsley, minced**
   - **1 small bay leaf (fresh or dry), minced**
   - **pinch of cumin seeds**
   - **pinch of salt**
   - **black pepper**

2. Refrigerate 1 hour. Serve in small earthenware pot with black bread on the side.

FRITTO DI RICOTTA

Fried Ricotta

10 1/2 oz. Ricotta	1 tablespoon
5 tablespoons flour	Acquavite or Rum
1 tablespoon sugar	Pure olive oil
Grated zest of 1 small lemon,	
or 1/2 orange	

1. Mix all ingredients well. Refrigerate 1 hour.

2. Heat a generous amount of pure olive oil in a large fryer; with a oil-greased ladle, spoon mixture into pan (grease ladle each time). Cook until Ricotta is golden brown on each side.

3. Sprinkle sparingly with sugar. Serve immediately.

BREAD AND CHEESE

See "Antipastos" Chapter, page 16.

BROAD BEANS AND CHEESE

See "Antipastos" Chapter, page 16.

CHEESE BALLS

See "Antipastos" Chapter, page 22.

Detail of the "Cantoria," a bass-relief by the Florentine Luca della Robbia. Museo del Duomo di Firenze (Florence).

Desserts

BUDINO DIPLOMATICO FREDDO

Cold Pudding

Unless otherwise specified, recipes in this book serve four people.

1 tablespoon Sultanas
  white raisin
3 1/2 oz. Savoiardi biscuits
  or Spongecake
Citron-rind
Raisins
Apricot jam

3 1/2 tablespoons sugar
2 egg yolks
3 tablespoons cake flour
4 cups milk, hot
Whipped cream
1/2 cup Cognac

1. Soak 1/2 tablespoon sugar and citron-rind in Cognac . Cut biscuits or spongecake into small pieces.

2. In a pudding mould, make a 3/4 inch layer of biscuits; sprinkle a few raisins, small pieces of citron-rinds; cover with 1 or 2 teaspoons of apricot jam.

3. In a small saucepan, mix 3 tablespoons sugar with egg yolks and flour; then blend in hot milk. Cook over moderate heat, stirring constantly with a wooden spoon until the soft custard coats the spoon.

4. Pour some of this cream over the layer of raisins and jam.

5. Alternate layers of biscuits and cream until the mould is filled.

6. End with a layer of cream.

7. Cool; then, refrigerate. Before serving, remove from mould; garnish with whipped cream.

ANANASSO ALLA PANNA

Pineapple with Cream   *Serves 3*

3 large slices pineapple,
   fresh or canned
3-4 tablespoons sugar
I cup cream

1/4 cup Kirsch, or Rum
2 oz. chocolate, unsweetened
2-3 tablespoons water

1. Cut pineapple into chunks, I inch thick; add sugar, 2-3 tablespoons of water and liquor, stirring. Place in a serving bowl. Pour cream over pineapple mixture; sprinkle with small chips of chocolate.

2. Refrigerate I hour before serving.

ANANASSO CON PANNA GELATA

Pineapple with Frozen Cream   *Serves I*

I large slice pineapple, fresh
I tablespoon (scant) sugar

I 1/2 tablespoon Kirsch, or Rum
1/4 cup fresh cream

1. Soak pineapple in sugar and liquor; chill.

2. Whip cream (do not add sugar); freeze about I hour. Remove 2 or 3 minutes before serving.

3. Before serving, drain pineapple; set on individual dessert dishes; decorate with frozen cream. Pour some of the pineapple juice over it.

BANANE AL WHISKY

Bananas with Whisky

5-6 bananas
Juice of 2 medium oranges
6 tablespoons sugar

4 tablespoons Whiskey
Butter
Cream

1. Buy bananas when just ripe; cut into thick slices.

2. Place in large buttered, oven-proof dish. Pour orange juice over bananas; sprinkle with sugar. Place in hot oven and cook 10-15 minutes.

3. Remove from oven. Heat a ladle of Whisky; light it and pour over bananas.

4. Serve flambé with frozen cream on the side.

BANANE FLAMBÉES

Bananas Flambé

4 large bananas, thinly sliced
1 oz. butter
2 tablespoons sugar

Juice of 1 large orange
3 tablespoons Cognac
Whipped cream

1. Buy bananas when just ripe.

2. Melt butter in a frypan; add bananas; sauté over high heat for 1 minute.

3. Sprinkle with sugar; add orange juice; cook until juice is reduced to half.

4. Pour in Cognac; heat 30 seconds; light it.

5. Serve flambé with whipped cream on the side.

COMPOSTA DI PERE ALL'ANTICA

Pears with Marsala

6-7 cooking pears
1 cup white wine
1/4 cup dry Marsala
6-7 tablespoons sugar

Pieces of candied orange peel
Juice of 1 lemon
Powdered cinnamon
Whipped cream
Fine biscuits

1. With a small sharp knife, peel the pears and cut into quarters; remove cores; cut into small, regular chunks; toss in cold water with juice of 1/2 lemon.

2. In a saucepan, pour white wine, Marsala, sugar and a pinch of cinnamon. Bring to a boil; add pears, drained of their juice. Cook over medium high heat until pears are just tender, but firm. Remove pears with a slotted spoon and place into a bowl.

3. Simmer wine-Marsala liquid until condensed to a syrupy consistency; pour over pears; add orange zest. Blend well.

4. Cool; serve with whipped cream and fine biscuits.

PERE RIPIENE DI GORGONZOLA

Pears Stuffed with Gorgonzola

4 small firm ripe pears
1 tablespoon lemon juice
2 oz. Gorgonzola cheese

2 tablespoons soft
  unsalted butter
2 tablespoons minced walnuts,
  pistachio or pine nuts

1. With a small sharp knife, peel pears and cut into half lengthwise, leaving stem attached to one of the pear halves. Remove cores and scoop a scant tablespoon of pulp out of each half. To prevent the fruit from turning brown, paint each section of pear inside and out with a pastry brush dipped in lemon juice.

2. Cream Gorgonzola and soften butter by beating them together against the side of a small bowl with a wooden spoon until they are soft and fluffy.

3. Fill hollows of pears with a 1 tablespoon of cheese-and-butter mixture; carefully press two halves of pear together again.

4. Roll pears in crushed nuts; arrange on a serving plate. Chill about 2 hours, or until cheese is firm.

PERE AL VINO

Pears with Wine

4 ripe pears
1 cup dry white wine
5 tablespoons sugar

Black-currant jelly
Pinch of powdered cinnamon
Whipped cream

Prepare this dish several hours before serving.

1. Cut pears into quarters; remove cores; peel; slice (not too thinly)

2. In a bowl, arrange pears, sprinkle with sugar and cinnamon; pour wine over pears; stir once; chill (do not disturb until ready to serve).

3. Arrange pears in individual cups; add a spoon of whipped cream; garnish with small balls of black-currant jelly.

COPPA "EVENING SMILE"

Cup of Evening Smile

4 eggs
4 tablespoons fine sugar

7 oz. whipped cream,
**   unsweetened**
1/4 cup Gin
Fine biscuits

1. Beat yolks with sugar; then, beat egg whites; when they are white and frothy, add to yolks; add whipped cream. Flavor with Gin. Mix gently. Refrigerate until ready to serve.

2. Serve in cups with fine biscuits on the side.

COPPA DI MASCARPONE

Mascarpone Cup

7 oz. Mascarpone cheese
2 eggs
Sugar, powdered
3 tablespoons of Cognac or Rum

Savoiardi biscuits or
   Spongecake
Candied cherries

1. Blend Mascarpone with egg yolks and sugar; add liquor.

2. Beat egg whites until fluffy; add creamed Mascarpone.

3. Soak Savoiardi or spongecake slices in liquor; place them in bottom of individual cups. Garnish with candied cherries. Refrigerate until ready to serve.

CREMA DI MASCARPONE

Cream of Mascarpone

5 oz. Mascarpone cheese
6 tablespoons fine sugar
2 egg yolks
1 egg white

4 slices spongecake
4 candied cherries
3 tablespoons of Rum

1. Whip yolks with sugar until they are light and frothy. Add Mascarpone a little bit at a time, beating briskly. Beat egg whites until stiff; add to Mascarpone slowly and carefully until firm. Add 1 1/2 tablespoon of Rum.

2. Arrange slices of spongecake in individual cups; add 1 tablespoon of Rum diluted with a little water; cover with Mascarpone cream. Chill 1/2 hour.

3. Soak candied cherries 1/2 hour in a 1/2 tablespoon of Rum. Before serving, decorate individual cups with cherries; sprinkle with candied cherry juice.

FRAGOLINE NICKILEIN

Strawberries Nickilein

14 oz. small strawberries
4 tablespoons sugar
4 tablespoons Maraschino liquor

1/2 teaspoon grated
orange zest
1 cup whipped cream,
unsweetened

1. In a small colander, wash strawberries under running water; drain well.

2. Arrange strawberries in a dessert goblet; sprinkle with sugar and grated orange zest; add Maraschino. Chill until ready to serve.

3. Serve covered with whipped cream, or serve cream on the side.

MELE AL FORNO (1)

Baked Apples (1)

Using ripe rennet apples, prepare as follows:

1. Wash apples; with a small sharp knife, cut apple tops; remove core; enlarge cavity.

2. In bottom of a baking pan, pour 3/4 inch of white wine, stirring in a bit of sugar.

3. Fill apples with apricot marmalade mixed with a handful of Amaretto crumbs and 1/2 cup of Cognac. Add more apricot marmalade and sprinkle sugar on top of apples.

4. Place in moderate oven and cook 45 minutes to 1 hour. Serve warm with whipped cream on the side.

FILLING VARIATIONS:
   a) Apricot marmalade, Cognac and slivered almonds.
   b) Orange marmalade, minced walnuts, honey, cinnamon.
   c) Chopped dates, minced walnuts, honey, cinnamon.

MELE IN FORNO (2)

Baked Apples (2)

5 rennet apples, medium, ripe
2 oz. butter
1 cup dry Marsala
A few drops of vanilla

1 handful pine nuts
6 tablespoons of sugar
Whipped cream

1. Peel apples; remove cores; cut into 8 pieces.

2. Over high heat, melt butter in a flame-proof casserole; when it is slightly brown, add apples; sauté, for 3-4 minutes, stirring twice.

3. Sprinkle with half the amount of sugar; add Marsala and a few drops of vanilla. Blend ingredients for 2 minutes. Place in a 350 degree oven.

4. After 10 minutes remove from oven and sprinkle apples with pine nuts and remaining sugar. Return to oven; raise temperature and cook 10-15 minutes, or until wine mixture is slightly candied.

5. Serve warm, with cold whipped cream on the side.

OMELETTE DI MELE

Apple Omelettes

5 or 6 rennet apples
4 tablespoons of Cognac
Sugar

Frying batter
Pure olive oil
1 egg white

1. Peel apples; remove core; cut into slices 1/4 inch thick.

2. Soak in Cognac and sugar for 1 hour.

3. Make a batter with 2 tablespoons of flour, 1/4 cup of cold water; mix until it is smooth and thick. Add a pinch of salt and 1 tablespoon of pure olive oil, mix well. Let stand for 1 hour.

4. Beat egg white to a frothy consistency and blend into batter. Fold apples into the batter, blend well; drop by spoonfuls into hot oil and fry until apples are golden brown on both sides.

CHARLOTTE ALLE MANDORLE
Almond Charlotte

1 tablespoon fine flour
1 qt. milk + 3 tablespoons
4 egg yolks
4 or 5 tablespoons sugar
1/4 teaspoon of vanilla
3 1/2 oz. almonds, slivered
  and minced

Savoiardi biscuits or
  spongecake sliced
Candied cherries
1/2 cup of butter
Cognac or Rum

1. Blend flour with 3 tablespoons of cold milk. Add egg yolks and 1 qt. cold milk, mix well; add sugar.

2. Cook over low heat, stirring constantly, until mixture is thick (do not boil!). Flavor with vanilla.

3. Remove from heat; add butter and stir until well blended; add almonds and stir well.

4. In a pudding mould, place a layer of Savoiardi or spongecake slices lightly soaked in liquor; pour in enough sauce to cover biscuits. Repeat this operation until mould is filled; finish with a layer of biscuits.

5. Refrigerate for 4 hours; remove from mould and garnish with cherries.

PANNA MONTATA IN SORPRESA
Whipped Cream Surprise

1. In individual cups, pour a layer of whipped cream; then arrange a slice of Angel cake soaked in a sauce with Cognac (see end of this chapter, "Sauces with Liquor").

2. Cover with a thin layer of apricot marmalade slightly thinned with Cognac; then, top with a generous amount of whipped cream. Sprinkle with cinnamon, and serve.

SCHIACCIATINE ALLE MANDORLE

Almond Cake   *Makes 30 small cakes*

10 1/2 oz. almonds, blanched, minced
9 oz. sugar, dissolved in water
Zest of 1 orange, grated (remove white skin)

1. In a tureen, blend almonds with sugar and orange zest, adding a few drops of water at a time to obtain a smooth dough.

2. Roll 1 teaspoon of mixture in the palms of your hands; make walnut-size balls; then press and flatten.

3. Arrange cakes in buttered oven proof dish; cook 20-30 minutes on low heat. Cake should not be dry nor brown.

PESCHE RIPIENE

Peaches with Macaroons   *Serves 6*

6 firm ripe peaches   **2 tablespoons sugar**
5 stale macaroons,   **4 tablespoons unsalted butter**
   crumbled in blender   **2 egg yolks**

1. Preheat oven to 375 degrees. Blanch peaches, 2 at a time, in boiling water for about 20 seconds. Lift them out with a slotted spoon, plunge them into cold water; peel skins with a small sharp knife.

2. Cut peaches in half, remove pits. Scoop enough pulp out of each half to make a deep space in the center. Add this pulp to crumbled macaroons; stir in sugar, butter and egg yolks.

3. Stuff peach halves with macaroons mixture. Arrange halves side by side in buttered 8 by 10 inch baking dish; bake in 300 degree oven for 25 minutes, or until just tender. Baste with sugar syrup from baking pan. Serve hot or cold.

SPUMONE DI PESCHE

Peach Spumoni

1 1/2 lb. peaches, peeled
5 oz. sugar
1/2 oz. Rum
1 envelope Knox gelatine

2 cups whipped cream,
   sweetened
Candied cherries
Touch of almond extract

1. Peel peaches; cut in pieces. Soak in 3 1/2 oz. sugar and 1/2 oz. of Rum. Purée through a sieve.

2. Add to purée remaining sugar, almond extract and gelatine (follow package instructions for preparation). Add whipped cream to mixture, blend well.

3. Pour purée into a mould; refrigerate for several hours.

4. Before serving, remove Spumoni from mould; garnish with whipped cream and cherries.

VARIATIONS
You can make a Spumoni dish with all kinds of fruit, including apricots mixed with banana.

PESCHE ALLA MELBA

Melba Peaches

1/2 peach in syrup per serving
Whipped cream, frozen

Raspberry syrup
Almonds, slivered, toasted

Place 1/2 peach in individual cups; top with cream; cover with raspberry syrup; sprinkle with almonds. Serve.

ZABAGLIONE

Custard with Marsala

5 egg yolks	**2 tablespoons sugar**
1 whole egg	**1/2 cup dry Marsala**

1. Combine yolks, whole egg and sugar in top of a double boiler above simmering water, or in a medium heat-proof glass bowl set in a shallow pan of barely simmering water.

2. Beat mixture with whisk or rotary beater until it is pale yellow and fluffy. Gradually add Marsala and continue beating until mixture becomes thick enough to hold its shape on a spoon (do not boil!). This process takes about 10 minutes.

3. Spoon zabaglione into individual bowls, or large glasses. Serve hot.

BACCHUS: *The Greek-Roman God of grape-growing and of wine. Painted by Caravaggio. Uffizi Gallery, Florence.*

SFORMATO DI AMARETTI E ZABAGLIONE
Zabaglione and Amaretti Pudding

3 oz. Amaretti biscuits
3 oz. sugar
3 oz. potato flour
3 eggs, separated

4 1/4 cups of milk
1 oz. butter
1/4 cup of Rum

1. In a small saucepan, blend sugar, flour and 4 cups of milk ; mix well with a wooden spoon.

2. On the side, soak Amaretti in a mixture of 1/4 cup of milk and 1/4 cup of Rum; let stand for 30 minutes.

3. Drain biscuits; purée through a sieve. Blend purée with the mixture of flour, sugar and milk.

4. Cook over moderate heat, stirring constantly with a wooden spoon until mixture is almost thick. Remove from heat and cool slightly.

5. Add egg yolks, mixing well; then add egg whites beaten until white and fluffy.

6. Grease a mould with butter; add mixture and place in oven to keep warm.

7. Prepare a Zabaglione cream (see "Zabaglione" recipe page 145).

8. Remove pudding from mould. Just before serving, pour warm Zabaglione cream over pudding. Serve warm.

IL DOLCE DEL PRELATO

Prelate's Cake

Spongecake, thinly sliced
5 oz. chocolate, unsweetened
2 oz. sugar
5 eggs
2 oz. butter

Vanilla, powdered
2 oz. candied orange, minced
1 cup of strong coffee,
    slightly sweetened
Snip of Rum

1. Soak slices of spongecake in strong coffee, slightly sweetened, and flavored with a snip of Rum. Place slices on sides and bottom of a square mould.

2. Prepare a chocolate foam in this way: Over low heat, blend chocolate in just enough water to dissolve it; remove from heat. Mix well egg yolks, sugar, a pinch of powdered vanilla, pieces of butter, a snip of Rum. Beat egg whites until white and firm; blend them and candied orange with chocolate. Blend chocolate with egg yolk mixture. Taste for flavor.

3. Pour this mousse into the mould with spongecake; make another layer of spongecake slices. Add more coffee; refrigerate for 24 hours. Garnish with whipped cream before serving.

ZUPPA INGLESE

English Soup

10 1/2 oz. Savoiardi biscuits, or Spongecake	Jam (any fruit)
	Candied fruit
3 1/2 oz. Marsala or Maraschino liquor	Cherries

FOR THE CREAM:

2 egg yolks	4 cups milk
2 tablespoons sugar	2 oz. sugar
1 teaspoon potato flour	

1. Prepare a cream in this way: In a saucepan, mix egg yolks with sugar and flour. Slowly, pour in hot milk, a little at a time, stirring constantly.

2. Cook over low heat; stir constantly with a wooden spoon (do not boil!). The cream is done when the spoon is covered with a smooth layer of cream.

3. In a deep serving dish, lay the biscuits hollow side down (or slices of spongecake). Pour in liquor; cover with a layer of jam, then a layer of cream. Repeat this operation ending with a layer of cream. Garnish with pieces of candied fruit and cherries.

SAUCE WITH LIQUOR

Prepare this sauce with 3 tablespoons of sugar dissolved in 8 oz. water and boiled 5 minutes. Remove from heat; season with a liquor. Cold, this cream can be used to soak slices or layers of cake.

Recipe Index

General Index